MASS INCARCERATION
ON TRIAL

Also by Jonathan Simon

Governing Through Crime

MASS INCARCERATION ON TRIAL

A Remarkable Court Decision and the Future of Prisons in America

JONATHAN SIMON

THE NEW PRESS

NEW YORK
LONDON

Requests for permission to reproduce selections from this book
should be mailed to: Permissions Department, The New Press, 120
Wall Street, 31st floor, New York, NY 10005.

Published in the United States by The New Press, New York, 2014
Distributed by Two Rivers Distribution

ISBN 978-1-62097-254-0 (pbk.)

LIBRARY OF CONGRESS CATALOGING-IN-PUBLICATION DATA
Simon, Jonathan, 1959– author.
    Mass incarceration on trial : a remarkable court decision and the
future of prisons in America / Jonathan Simon.
        pages cm
    Includes bibliographical references and index.
    ISBN 978-1-59558-769-5 (hardback) — ISBN 978-1-59558-792-3
(e-book) 1. Prisons— Law and legislation— United States.
2. Correctional law— United States. 3. Administration of
criminal justice— United States. 4. Punishment— Law and
legislation— United States. I. Title.
    KF9730.S56 2014
    344.7303'5—dc23
                                                2013045415

The New Press publishes books that promote and enrich public
discussion and understanding of the issues vital to our democracy
and to a more equitable world. These books are made possible by
the enthusiasm of our readers; the support of a committed group
of donors, large and small; the collaboration of our many partners
in the independent media and the not-for-profit sector; booksellers,
who often hand-sell New Press books; librarians; and above all by
our authors.

www.thenewpress.com

Composition by Westchester Book Composition
This book was set in Palatino

Printed in the United States of America

This book is dedicated to my mother, Marlene Bragman
Simon, whose passion for confronting social problems
and seeking social justice has always served
as a beacon for my research

Contents

Acknowledgments

The author is grateful for the comments on some or all of the manuscript from Jed Bickman, Andrew Coyle, Ian Cummings, Malcolm Feeley, Ruth Gilmore, Richard Jones, Shadd Maruna, Kieran McEvoy, Tony Platt, Marlene Simon, Richard Sparks, Diane Wachtell, and Frank Zimring. As always, all failures of fact and interpretation belong solely to the author.

MASS INCARCERATION
ON TRIAL

Introduction

Inhuman Punishment

Like a biblical flood, the age of mass incarceration is finally ebbing. After forty years—not forty days—a once unstoppable tide of harsh sentencing laws, aggressive prosecution policies, and diminished opportunities for parole seems to be subsiding. Today the number of people imprisoned in America remains at or near historic highs (nearly four times the average incarceration rate for the first three quarters of the twentieth century), but the quantitative trend is modestly downward.[1] States have begun to modify some of the most extreme sentencing laws, including New York's infamous Rockefeller Drug Laws, which created life sentences for first-time possession of modest quantities of drugs for sale, and once impossible discussions of alternatives to routine imprisonment for many drug and property crimes are beginning to take place at the state level.

But although the levels have stopped rising, the flood of mass incarceration is still upon us, and the effects of what has been done remain, largely below the surface. Beyond the numbers, the quantitative story of mass incarceration,[2] we as a society know shockingly little about what this far-from-natural disaster has wrought, the qualitative story of mass incarceration.[3] What kind of prisons has it produced? What kinds of prisoners do they hold? Is imprisonment necessary to sustain lower crime levels? Without answers to such questions, it will be impossible to rebalance and restore an American criminal justice system that has, in the view of one its sharpest observers, William Stuntz, "collapsed."[4]

Despite being a specialist in the study of punishment and society, even an early identifier of some of the critical features that have come to define mass incarceration,[5] I did not know enough to ask these questions, let alone begin to think about answering them, until the end of the last decade, some thirty-five years into the age of mass incarceration and a quarter century after I had begun to study it. The source of this late insight was an unusual federal trial held before a special three-judge court in 2009. That case, *Coleman-Plata v. Schwarzenegger*, was a consolidation of two independent but related ongoing federal court cases covering California prisons: *Coleman v. Wilson*, a 1995 case ordering comprehensive improvements to mental health care delivery in prisons, and *Plata v. Davis*, a 2002 negotiated agreement in which California admitted systemwide violations of its constitutional requirement to provide adequate medical care in its prison system. This litigation revealed a depth of depravity in California's prisons that most academic critics, including me, had not imagined. When the Supreme Court reviewed the California decision, the result was a resounding legal victory for prisoners. The majority opinion in *Brown v. Plata* drew a direct line between the sentencing practices of mass incarceration and the inhumane conditions in prisons—the quantitative and qualitative stories. The majority, while only one vote strong, powerfully proclaimed the human dignity of prisoners and the requirement to provide humane conditions as core animating values of constitutional punishment.

This book attempts to use the California court decisions leading up to and including *Brown v. Plata* to show the way toward a legal dismantling of mass incarceration. If, as those cases cumulatively seem to imply, imprisonment on the scale that currently exists in California is fundamentally incompatible with humane conditions, if the physical and mental health requirements of prisoners cannot be constitutionally met on a mass scale, then mass incarceration is inherently unconstitutional. It is therefore incumbent on us—and constitutionally required—to examine and change our use of incarceration as the primary response to crime.

*   *   *

The term *mass incarceration* was first used by specialists in the field of punishment and society to describe the tremendous changes in the scale of incarceration that began in the late 1970s and became visible to readers of imprisonment charts by the middle of the 1980s.[6] In time, these specialists and community activists voiced a long list of criticisms of mass incarceration, including racial disproportionality,[7] high collateral costs to the communities of highest incarceration,[8] and the very debatable effect of imprisonment in reducing violence—the chief concern in actual high-crime communities.[9] Twenty-five years later, these critiques have begun to gain some traction politically, boosted by the recent economic crisis that has forced state political leaders to consider cuts even to the once sacrosanct correctional budget, as well as by the happier fact that most of the very significant crime reductions throughout the United States during the 1990s have so far been sustained despite the hard economic times.

It remains to be seen, however, if these trends by themselves can drive a sustained reduction in incarceration rates. Many of the laws and policies that produced mass incarceration remain firmly in place. More important, so do the habituated responses of the media, politicians, and ordinary citizens—what I call with some irony our "common sense" about prisons, prisoners, and crime prevention. A recovering economy combined with a surge in levels of urban crime could restore the flood of prisoners, which, after decades of growing prison populations, often feels "normal."[10]

For all the powerful and damning labels that have been laid on it—"the prison industrial complex," "the human waste management system," and most recently and perhaps most memorably, the new Jim Crow—mass incarceration retains legitimacy among people in general and the legal elites (judges, legislators, prosecutors) most likely to influence its immediate course. The claim that it keeps the "innocent" safe from the "guilty" sounds glib and inherently contradictory to those of us who are familiar with the social realities of criminal victimization, but it is neither obviously spurious nor, broadly speaking, disingenuous. In the words of a legal decision, *Spain v. Procunier*, that has become a talisman for the legitimacy of mass incarceration in the federal courts, prisons keep "dangerous men in safe custody under humane conditions."[11]

Mass incarceration, however, defies all three of the promises implicit in the *Spain* decision. Imprisonment on the scale currently practiced by the United States has meant that literally millions of people *who are not dangerous* have nonetheless been locked up for many years. Furthermore, given the record levels of physical and sexual violence prevalent in our prisons today, it is deceitful to argue that the custody provided prisoners is "safe." And finally, perhaps most important, we do not have the capacity to deal with the physical and mental health requirements of a prison population four times larger than historical levels, a higher percentage of our population than that of any other country on the planet, so the conditions existing in U.S. prisons today are fundamentally, irreparably inhumane.[12] Therefore mass incarceration does not and cannot comport with the Eighth Amendment's prohibition of "cruel and un-usual" punishment.

Even to many specialists, the inhumanity of our prisons, es-pecially their lack of health care, came as a surprise.[13] This was not entirely our fault. Prison administrations during the era of mass incarceration have become insular and resistant to docu-mentation by journalists, social scientists, or human rights ex-perts, making it far more difficult to know beyond anecdote and urban legend how bad things had become inside. In the 1970s, prisons borrowed freely from the "medical model," designed to emphasize classification of prisoners based on individualized knowledge of them and access to therapeutic programs. Al-though sometimes based in an antiquated physical infrastruc-ture, the penal regime had a variety of incentives to promote the well-being of individual prisoners, especially their mental health. Wealthier states provided generally good and some-times excellent medical care to prisoners (although troubling experiments went on as well).[14] For the most part, prisoners were young, fit, and not there for very long. Poorer states, espe-cially those in the South and West, found themselves under pressing judicial demands to improve their prisoners' physical and medical situation.[15] A new stock of prisons in the 1980s built to modern, judicially established standards created a presump-tion shared even by critics of mass incarceration that prisons were at least secure and humane. California built more than twenty new prisons during the 1980s and 1990s, the last one of this era coming into use in 2004).

Yet a variety of factors created conditions in the new prisons far worse than anyone on the outside imagined—except, of course, members of prisoners' and prison officers' families, prisoner-rights lawyers, and the formerly incarcerated. First, re-habilitation was out of fashion as a justification for imprison-ment, and while all too many assumed a rehabilitative approach would continue to inform penal practice, administrators of the new prisons showed a crass disregard not just for rehabilitative treatment but for humane treatment. Given a warrant to build vast new modern prison systems, prison planners in the 1980s prioritized capacity, especially for high-security custody. The new prisons were designed to be overcrowded and locked down. Screening for serious mental and medical problems was not a priority, seldom even a consideration. The new prisons of mass incarceration were built with a shocking lack of planning for providing for human needs, particularly medical and mental health services.

Second, the prison population became older. As sentencing policies changed to encourage imprisonment of persistent minor offenders, who were often drug addicts or mentally ill, sentences lasted much longer, parole policies created a revolving door between parole and prison, and the burden of ill health within the prison population grew. These changes created an increasingly "geriatric" prison population with a much higher burden of chronic illness, including mental illness, than in the past, when prisoners came mostly from a class of professional criminals.

Third, arrest and plea-bargain policies have led to drastic overcrowding. (This overcrowding was clearly foreseen, as the new prisons were designed with plumbing and electrical capacity for up to double the normal population for sustained periods of time.) Overcrowding in turn led to a need for behavioral controls, including frequent lockdowns and long-term solitary confinement for many prisoners. And incarceration on a mass scale decreased prisons' ability to provide programs or training to break the monotony of time in the cell and to prepare prisoners for reentry; this in turn led to higher recidivism rates, which further inflated the prison population.

The result, largely invisible until the past decade, was a toxic cocktail: an epidemic of chronic disease and mental illness among prisoners combined with permanent hyper-overcrowding in prisons designed with deliberate indifference to the humanity of their occupants. Not every state is approaching California's level of inhumanity, but atrocious prison conditions are widespread, and their true extent remains hidden by self-protecting correctional bureaucracies and complacent media used to covering "crime" and "criminals," not mass incarceration. The quantitative explosion of prison populations and the qualitative implosion in the security and humanity of our prisons are related, but their stories have remained largely apart, with scholars of punishment tracing the quantitative trends, while prisoners' legal advocates have focused on the abysmal and dangerous conditions in prisons. In 2009 a special three-judge federal court in a case then titled *Coleman v. Schwarzenegger* (after the older of the two underlying cases and governor Arnold Schwarzenegger) held a fourteen-day hearing that finally brought the two stories together and placed mass incarceration on trial. In August 2009, the three-judge federal court issued an opinion finding that California's chronic levels of hyper-overcrowding prevent any possibility of correcting the unconstitutional lack of mental and physical health care that had persisted despite two decades of court orders to remedy it.[16] The court held that the nearly 200 percent overcrowding in the system during that period (300 percent more common in the reception centers, where most short-term prisoners languish) had made any adequate remedy to unconstitutional health conditions impossible. The judges ordered the state to reduce the overcrowding to 137 percent in two years, a reduction of approximately forty thousand prisoners from the population at the time of the hearing.[17]

Coleman v. Schwarzenegger in 2009 and the Supreme Court's review in *Brown v. Plata* in 2011 reveal in a more integrated way the size and nature of mass incarceration. These cases show that California built prisons heedless of the humanity of those it planned to incarcerate, recklessly accumulated people with chronic illnesses in those prisons, and committed itself to an extreme penal philosophy that left the state unable to address the inevitable suffering and death. The results were atrocious enough to move even a Supreme Court long tolerant of mass incarceration. In the words of Justice Kennedy's majority opinion in *Brown*:

> Just as a prisoner may starve if not fed, he or she may suffer or die if not provided adequate medical care. A prison that deprives prisoners of basic sustenance, including adequate medical care, is incompatible with the concept of human dignity and has no place in civilized society.[18]

The fact that this was a principle of long standing made the decision no less dramatic. For more than twenty years, the high court had used its rare legal reviews of prison cases mostly to instruct lower courts on the deference owed to state penological choices and the expertise of state prison administrators. Prisoners had plenty of theoretical rights "on the books," mostly applications of the Eighth Amendment's prohibition of cruel and unusual punishment, but trial courts following the Supreme Court's instructions could see incarceration only "through a glass darkly," the realities of prison life distanced and white-washed. In *Brown v. Plata*, the court seemed at some pains to send a different, opposite signal.

> If government fails to fulfill this obligation, the courts have a responsibility to remedy the resulting Eighth Amendment violation. . . . Courts must be sensitive to the State's interest in punishment, deterrence, and rehabilitation, as well as the need for deference to experienced and expert prison administrators faced with the difficult and dangerous task of housing large numbers of convicted criminals. . . . Courts nevertheless must not shrink from their obligation to "enforce the constitutional rights of all 'persons,' including

prisoners." . . . Courts may not allow constitutional violations to continue simply because a remedy would involve
intrusion into the realm of prison administration.[19]

The appeal turned on a technical issue, whether the three-
judge court had given sufficient weight to public safety as required by the Prison Litigation Reform Act before a court may
set a prison population cap. In affirming the lower court's order
to drastically reduce California's prison population, the Supreme Court complemented its broad call for the human rights
of prisoners with recognition of the close examination of crime
risk undertaken by the trial court. Justice Kennedy's majority
opinion departed substantially from the presumption of dangerousness commonly projected onto all felons by agreeing
with the trial court that California could divert many felons
currently being sent to prison without endangering public
safety. (The alarming "common sense" about felons, however,
was vividly represented by Justice Alito's dissent, in which he
asserted that the majority ruling would result in "the premature release of approximately 46,000 criminals—the equivalent
of three Army divisions.")[20]

*   *   *

Brown v. Plata and the cases that led up to it teach a powerful
lesson about our recent experiment with mass incarceration, a
lesson that has the potential to reshape American imprisonment: human dignity and public safety go together; one cannot flourish without the other. California's uncompromising
use of imprisonment in a bid to reduce the risk of violence to
the public and prison officers has produced prisons of extreme
peril. Ignoring their wards' humanity, prison managers lost the
ability to understand and intervene to benefit their individual
inmates. Without that understanding and ability, imprisonment became a kind of torture for those suffering from physical

or mental illnesses, creating a level of neglect that was cruel and unusual as well as inhumane.

For many, the question of whether our prisons honor human dignity may seem secondary to the racial disproportionality of mass incarceration.[21] But the two issues are deeply intertwined, and our understanding of both will be strengthened if we bring them together. In our time, racial profiling is a way of denying a person's dignity by being treated as a member of a class, not an individual human being. Moreover, the inhumanity in our prisons is a legacy of slavery's comprehensive practices of degradation and punishment, which has left its mark on American penology from the plantation prisons of Jim Crow to the warehouses of mass incarceration.[22] Likewise, the racialization of the prison population, which may have begun before the period of mass incarceration but increased greatly during it, has made it easier to keep the inhumanity of prisons invisible to the majority of Americans. By the same token, reforms aimed at reducing the most racially unfair sentencing laws but leave prisons themselves massively overcrowded and inhumane will not end the moral shame of mass incarceration.

With legal recognition of prisoners' human rights come responsibilities. A turning point has been reached in the history of American imprisonment. We will either decide to countenance inhumane and degrading treatment on an industrial scale, or we will have to rethink our approach to crime and punishment, beginning with downsizing and radically reinventing prisons.

This book is a reading of the decisions in the series of federal court challenges to the health conditions of California prisoners that culminated in *Brown v. Plata*. These decisions are legal precedents with ongoing relevance to prison lawyers and officials, but they are also a public sociology text, addressed to all of us, concerning the threat that mass incarceration poses to prisoners, prison officers, and any society with pretensions to decency.

Chapter 1 provides the historical background of California's extreme path. The policies California put in place were not just "tough on crime" in the sense that had already become generic in the late 1960s; they reflected a historically distinct experience of fear of crime anchored in the social and economic transformations of the 1970s.[23] Prison came to be seen as the only reliable way to prevent crime, resulting in a strategy I call *total incapacitation*[24] to distinguish it from the traditional use of imprisonment as a dignified effort to defend society against crime. Once in place, this new logic of imprisonment produced a zero-sum contest between the dignity of prisoners and public safety, which promoted deliberate indifference to the needs of prisoners, from physical and mental health care needs to the need for decent accommodation free from overcrowding and other forms of cruel and unusual punishment.

Chapter 2 looks at *Madrid v. Gomez*, a case filed by the same lawyers and decided at virtually the same time as *Coleman v. Wilson*, the first part of the *Brown v. Plata* litigation. *Madrid* was a landmark challenge to supermax-style incarceration and California's extreme version of total isolation. A supermax,[25] officially dubbed a Security Housing Unit in California, replaces all activities with a twenty-three-hour lockdown of prisoners in their cells. Not even prison officers interact with a prisoner more than it takes to shove a tray through a narrow slot. This style was not invented in California, but it was embraced enthusiastically as the state responded to nightmares of the 1970s with two giant supermax prisons, each holding more than a thousand prisoners.[26]

The *Madrid* opinion opened a window on shocking supermax practices. Prisons that were supposed to represent a technologically sophisticated approach to reducing violence from highly dangerous prisoners looked more like medieval punishments of the mentally ill. Judge Thelton Henderson's opinion in *Madrid* offered stinging criticism of the supermax strategy, but it was only a partial victory for prisoners. Following Supreme Court precedent to defer broadly to California's total incapacitation logic, Judge Henderson stopped just short of finding the supermax to be inherently "cruel and unusual" and thus a violation of the Eighth Amendment, instead ordering major changes in the internal security procedures of the prison. Most significantly for our subject, Judge Henderson did hold that housing prisoners with a serious mental illness in a Security Housing Unit does violate the Eighth Amendment.

Although California's supermax strategy and its commitment to total incapacitation survived this legal challenge, the court's characterization of the state's stance toward mentally ill prisoners as "deliberate indifference" revealed a major legal and moral vulnerability. *Madrid* was one of the first decisions to recognize the chronic-illness problem inherent in the new prisons. It was also the first case to suggest how far an argument focused on dignity and rooted in the Eighth Amendment might go forward confronting mass incarceration.

Chapter 3 looks at the first of two cases that broadened the health-based attack on mass incarceration from the supermax to the general prison population. *Coleman v. Wilson*[27] unfolded nearly in tandem with *Madrid*, and the opinion was clearly influenced by Judge Henderson's opinion in that case. *Coleman* revealed that California held approximately 15,000 prisoners with serious mental illness, while its growing collection of prisons lacked any minimally adequate mental health treatment. Judge Lawrence Karlton of the U.S. District Court for the Eastern District of California found that the state's systematic failure to treat mentally ill prisoners in the general prison population—let alone those in total isolation—constituted "deliberate indifference" to the serious danger faced and posed by those prisoners and thus violated the Eighth Amendment. Judge Karlton appointed a special master to oversee a massive reform in the way the Department of Corrections delivered mental health care. A decade after the decision, in 2006, the number of prisoners in the *Coleman* class (a conservative estimate of the actual number of mentally ill prisoners in California prisons) had reached 35,000 while the special master's reports indicated only modest progress in implementing the reform.

Coleman began to undermine the presumed moral foundations of mass incarceration by exposing its inhumanity. Moreover, it challenged the premise that dangerousness is an *unchanging* characteristic of all prisoners. For prisoners with a serious mental illness, *change* in prison takes the predictable form of *decompensation*, the clinical term for the deepening of a mental illness due to the lack of treatment or activities that might otherwise offset or compensate for the psychological issues. The failure of health care to identify and diagnose mental illness and then deliver necessary treatments makes mentally ill prisoners more dangerous once released.[28]

Chapter 4 follows California's experiment in mass incarceration to the turn of the twenty-first century as the *Coleman* health-and-humanity legal challenge was expanded to the entire medical-care system in California prisons. *Plata v. Davis*[29] revealed that all California prisoners are at real risk of serious harm or death if they ever need significant medical care in prison. The *Plata* complaint reads like a list of cases in a county hospital, as if to underscore the fact that prisoners, for all they may have done, are in the end human beings, with knees that break down, and kidneys and hearts that fail.

The stories also reveal a historic change in the biological challenge of incarceration. Designed in the eighteenth century to prevent the ravages of contagious diseases such as "jail fever" (typhus), the cellular prison still common today is increasingly struggling with a new health threat, chronic illnesses. The long chain of causation and the relentless incremental progress of diseases like diabetes, cancer, AIDS, and mental illnesses, including schizophrenia and bipolar disorder, make them difficult to prevent and costly to treat. Chronic illness cannot be checked or contained with the traditional methods of hygiene, quarantine, and vaccine, at which prisons (at least in principle) can excel. Effective treatment requires complex, precise, individualized, and consistent regimes of both medication and behavioral changes—methods well beyond the capacity of prisons generally and mass-incarceration prisons in particular. In the absence of effective treatment, chronic illnesses often do not typically cause immediate suffering or rapid death but generate high levels of future suffering and medical costs. The *Plata* record, replete with profile after profile of prisoners dying from routinized medical failure, provided unquestionable evidence of California's inability to attend to individual health care needs and the resulting degradation of prisoners' bodies. Their litigation records become many prisoners' only medical records, returning to them at least the possibility of being treated as individuals.

Chapter 5 looks at the first decade of the twenty-first century, as California continued to grow its prison population despite participating in a nationwide crime decline. Progress on the massive reform orders in *Coleman* and *Plata* remained largely stalled due to extreme levels of overcrowding in the entire prison system. For much of the previous decade, the California prison system had been operating at 200 to 300 percent of design capacity. This period of chronic hyper-overcrowding transformed California prisons into an unprecedented regime of incarceration. Lawyers for *Coleman* and *Plata* prisoners went back to court seeking a reduction in California's overcrowding as necessary to achieve the remedies. The combined *Coleman-Plata* case would be by far the largest and most systematic court intervention in U.S. prison history.[30]

The resulting trial and the order of the special three-judge court (which included Judge Henderson of the *Plata* case and Judge Karlton of *Coleman*) put mass incarceration on trial and opened a new chapter in the history of court reform of prisons. Holding that California's policies of routine imprisonment for low-level felonies and parole violations were largely to blame for the state's failure to create constitutionally adequate health care in its prisons, the court ordered California to reduce over-crowding to a level calculated carefully by the court to achieve progress on resolving the health care crisis while leaving the state as much leeway as possible to implement its strong pref-erence for imprisoning all felons: exactly 137 percent of design capacity within two years. While the court left the state free to meet that target through a rapid program of constructing new prisons, it was clear to all that the new level of imprisonment could practically be achieved only through drawing the prison population down by approximately forty thousand prisoners.

Chapter 6 follows California's appeal of that decision to the Supreme Court. In *Brown v. Plata*, a five-to-four majority voted to uphold the population-reduction order in its entirety. Al-though the court was divided, Justice Anthony Kennedy's ma-jority opinion was anything but narrow and offered a green light to begin what Justice Antonin Scalia in dissent called "the most radical injunction in our nation's history." *Brown* is the first major court-ordered reform of a state prison system since the Prison Litigation Reform Act of 1996 sought to close the doors of federal courts to prisoners.[31] Justice Kennedy's opinion also offered some of the strongest language in decades about pris-oners as more than legal subjects, possessors of "human dig-nity" whose recognition and protection "animates" the Eighth Amendment. The majority affirmed that it understood the in-humanity of California's prisons and appended three remark-able photographs of inhuman prison conditions to underscore its point. *Brown*'s emphasis on the human dignity of prisoners is a crucial new judicial contribution toward a better future for

American imprisonment. Realizing that promise requires us to recognize the humanitarian crisis created by California's commitment to total incapacitation. And, I argue, dignity provides the legal basis for nationwide dismantling of mass incarceration.[32]

As the trend of mass incarceration took hold in the 1970s, common sense all along the political spectrum held that prisons were a humane way to prevent crime by keeping a largely incorrigible population safely separated from the general public. The current crisis of mass incarceration does not by itself guarantee a meaningful reform, especially so long as these powerful assumptions about prisons, prisoners, and crime prevention, in place since the "fear years" of the 1970s, remain unchallenged. The conclusion of this book contests those assumptions by outlining a new common sense about prisons, prisoners, and crime prevention that is emerging as a direct response to mass incarceration.

1

Total Incapacitation

The 1970s and the Birth of an Extreme Penology

To appreciate the limits and potential of California's *Brown* case and the problem of inhumanity in prisons, it is important to recognize that California is to incarceration what Mississippi was to segregation—the state that most exemplifies the social and legal deformities of the practice. Although Californians are often reassured by their leaders that the state's current imprisonment rate is at or slightly below the national average, that argument conceals the significance of the increase in California's incarceration rates since 1980. It also glosses over the role of the Southern states, with their historically high rates and racist patterns of imprisonment, in setting the national average in the first place.

Between 1977 and 1995, states everywhere in the United States grew their prison populations, albeit at different paces. The causes are not mysterious: states decided as a matter of public policy to increase imprisonment.[1] More prisons for more people more of the time became a bipartisan consensus as the preferred solution to a raft of social problems, especially those associated with the economically poor urban neighborhoods that had high concentrations of minorities and immigrants. The rate of imprisonment, typically expressed as the number imprisoned per 100,000 population, quadrupled nationally from 117 in 1977 to 464 in 2009. In California, the rate went from 88 in 1977 to 478 in 2009, one of the highest swings in the nation. In absolute terms, California went from having fewer than 20,000 prisoners in 1977 to nearly 100,000 in 1990 and nearly 160,000 by 2003.

In qualitative terms, California began the 1970s as home to the nation's (and arguably one of the world's) most progressive correctional systems and one of the least reliant on imprisonment to deal with felony crime. From World War II through the early 1970s, under Democratic and Republican governors, California forged an evidence-based approach to rehabilitating prisoners that was second perhaps only to the Federal Bureau of Prisons in its fealty to a rehabilitative model. Starting in the late 1970s, however, California shifted toward total incapacitation. If *mass incarceration* describes a prison system grown to many times its normal scale, *total incapacitation* describes the rationale—often spelled out in slogans like "Use a gun and you're done" or "Three strikes and you're out"—that allows a criminal justice system to produce and sustain that condition.

Long-term regional patterns in imprisonment remained constant from the end of Reconstruction to the end of the 1970s. The South had the largest per capita prison population and the Northeast the smallest, with the West and Midwest in between. Thirty years of mass incarceration have shifted that lineup only a little: the West surpassed the Midwest as runner-up to the South. However, when California—far more populous than any other state in the Union—is considered as a region in itself, a more dramatic shift emerges. With 83 prisoners per 100,000 adult residents in 1977, California had an imprisonment rate slightly higher than the Northeast's, well below the

State Correctional Facility Incarceration Rates: 1977 and 2009

Source: Bureau of Justice Statistics, National Prisoner Statistics 1a, and National Prisoner Data Series: June 2009, December 1977; U.S. Census Bureau.

Midwest's, and just over half that of the South. In 2009, although a bit below its peak incarceration levels of 2006–7, California was the second most punitive region in the nation; its imprisonment rate was significantly higher than that of the Northeast and Midwest, and 80 percent that of the bellwether South. In terms of carceral geography, California moved from the progressive Midwest, à la Michigan or Minnesota, to the regressive South, at the level of Alabama or Arkansas, by the end of the 1990s. No other large state's imprisonment rate increased as much as California's—a staggering 500 percent between 1977 and 1998.[2]

This transformation was accomplished by changes in two different institutional systems. First, prosecutors and courts at the county level began to use the discretion built into the penal code to seek prison sentences in cases where probation had been more usual. The shift from probation to imprisonment

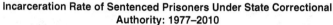

Incarceration Rate of Sentenced Prisoners Under State Correctional Authority: 1977–2010

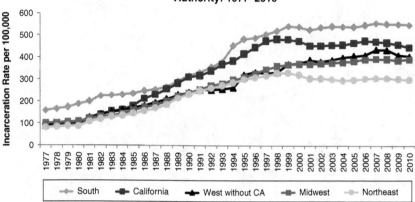

Source: Paige M. Harrison, *Prisoners in Custody of State or Federal Correctional Authorities, 1977–1998* (Washington, DC: Bureau of Justice Statistics, 2000), www.bjs.gov/index.cfm?ty=pbdetail&iid=2080 (accessed Nov. 19, 2013); Office of Justice Programs, *Sourcebook of Criminal Justice Statistics,* 1981 and 1984 (Washington, DC: Bureau of Justice Statistics, 1982 and 1985); and U.S. Census Bureau, 1980, 1990, 2000, 2010, with intercensal estimates by region, 2000–2010, and intercensal estimates for California, 1980–2010.

became more powerful as legislatures repeatedly amended the laws to lengthen terms and add harsher sentences.

Second, at the state level, executives and the legislatures cooperated to launch an epic program of prison construction, without which the courts might have tempered their sentencing in the early 1980s as overcrowding soared. In the century and a quarter between statehood in 1851 and 1980, California had built twelve prisons. Over the next two decades, between 1980 and 2000, twenty-two more prisons were added, most of them colossally larger than their predecessors. Even that building program did not keep up with the prodigious rate at which California imprisoned and reimprisoned its residents. By the end of the 1990s, chronic overcrowding was reaching crisis level—nearly 200 percent of an already inflated definition of capacity, despite a historic drop in crime.[3]

What happened to transform California from a state with a modest-size prison system and a slight bias against labeling people as felons and imprisoning them to a gargantuan system with an overwhelming bias *toward* labeling and imprisoning felons? The precise causes of the shift remain contested. What emerged following the shift was a new way of thinking about prisons, prisoners, and crime prevention that settled into a common sense during the 1970s. Many factors played a role in resetting California toward an extreme preference for incarceration including roles of courts, correctional officers' unions, politicians, the media, and homeowner voters, but the new common sense would lock the state's political establishment on a course toward a particularly inhumane and degrading form of mass incarceration.[4]

*   *   *

Mass incarceration's aura of legitimacy proceeds from its moral claim to protect the innocent from the guilty and from a lingering emotional response to the fears of the 1970s. Its emotional "truth" is frozen in the decade's nightmarish images, which continue to shape opinions about prisons, prisoners, and crime prevention long after the historical context has disappeared. For prisons and penal policy, as in so much of U.S. political life, the 1970s were a decisive decade. If the 1960s were years of hope interspersed with days of rage,[5] the 1970s were years of fear marked by days of horror. It's not that the decade lacked levity—indeed, a certain silliness—or that its economic problems look so bad in retrospect, but the 1970s began under shadows of national decline at home and abroad. Violent crime was increasing, the president and vice president were crooks who resigned to avoid prosecution, America's aggression in Southeast

Asia had killed 5 million people, and U.S. overthrow of progressive regimes and installation of brutal tyrants in Iran, Guatemala, the Congo, Chile, and elsewhere had led to widespread disgust. The 1970s were years of narrowing horizons and loss of national confidence.

Domestically, despite a leveling off or a downturn in homicides in many states by the end of the decade, mainstream culture in the 1970s built on the growing national narrative of crime fear. The late 1960s and early 1970s were punctuated by a series of high-profile mass or serial killings fueled by drugs, mental illness, sexual perversions, or all of the above, seemingly unchecked by a shrinking prison and public hospital system. Early in the decade, amid nationwide political turmoil generated by the ongoing Vietnam conflict, several high-profile prison uprisings resulted in the deaths of prison officers and prisoners and generated outsize nationwide revulsion (some of it manufactured by false reporting, such as the claim that prisoners had castrated one hostage and slit the throats of others). In California, which saw homicides continue to rise throughout the decade, all of these trends were magnified by a hypertrophic media industry and a tendency toward manic swings in self-image.[6]

Sociologists have recognized that the "common sense" produced by the experience of high crime rates in advanced industrial societies such as the United States and the United Kingdom produces support for "tough on crime" policies.[7] Fortunately, the way this common sense shapes policy has lately been studied in detail.[8]

Californians in the 1970s were not the first people in history to be worried about crime or to have a new and alarming picture of the risk of being a victim of it. What was distinct, however, was the degree to which this fear was transmitted directly into penal law and penal policy. At other times in U.S. history, the popular common sense about prisons, prisoners, and crime actually functioned as an important *constraint* on what was already a generally more progressive criminal justice policy. The "heating up" of penal politics in the 1970s[9]—particularly acute in California, with its tradition of citizen lawmaking through ballot initiatives[10]—resulted in a mind-set about crime, prisoners, and prisons that became "baked into" the state's penal policies.

First, according to the prevailing wisdom, most criminals have a high and unchanging potential for criminal activity, including violence, even if their present offense is not violent. Second, prison can do little to change criminals for the better, but prison can prevent them from endangering innocent people by keeping criminals locked up. Third, so-called penal experts cannot predict which criminals pose the most danger, so long sentences should be given to all. Fourth, any time a criminal leaves prison for any reason, the community becomes less safe.

As early as the last years of the 1970s, California prosecutors, who were politically the closest to the emerging common sense about crime and prisons, had already begun to implement an agenda of total incapacitation by using their broad discretion to bring the most serious of possible charges so as to obtain longer sentences. By the time new statutes lengthening sentences began to accumulate in the 1980s, they were piling onto already harsh new practice norms.[11] As a result, California incarceration patterns have little or no relationship to crime trends. Crime began to go down in the early 1980s, even before most tough-on-crime legislation was adopted. It grew again in the late 1980s as the crack-cocaine epidemic hit large cities including Los Angeles and Oakland, reaching a peak in the early 1990s, then began to decline before the adoption of even more virulent laws including "three strikes and you're out." Since then, the entire nation has experienced a sustained drop in crime, but it has been markedly shallower in California than in other states less committed to mass imprisonment.[12]

*   *   *

The common sense about prisons makes California's mass incarceration immune to conservative efforts to curtail spending and regulation, to liberal moves toward humane reform, and even to significant evidence of its failure to reduce crime. High rates of imprisonment remain entrenched even during a time of catastrophically low public revenues and high unemployment, whether crime rates are going up or down. In California, nothing more than tinkering at the edges of mass incarceration is likely to occur until the false assumptions supporting it are publicly disproved.

Our common sense about crime and punishment, like our other social "imaginaries," as the philosopher Charles Taylor notes, is "often not expressed in theoretical terms" but instead is "carried in images, stories and legends."[13] This makes the common-sense viewpoint very hard to fight with policy analysis and empirical social science, but it does not make it invulnerable. Such imaginaries carry with them, according to Taylor, "an idea of how [things] ought to go, of what missteps would invalidate the practice."[14] The most promising aspect of the legal crisis of prisons in California, and the medical humanitarian crisis behind it, is precisely the ability of the stories told in court to challenge this entrenched common sense with new characterizations and lessons that bring into question the morality and legitimacy of mass incarceration.

The criminal justice narrative embraced by California in the 1970s was based on a paradigm well suited to California's new economy as a rapidly upgrading suburban homeowner society: the citizen homeowner versus the predatory criminal intent on invading the home and doing violence to the family. Around this primal fear, several important story lines emerged in the 1970s, all emphasizing the vulnerability of victims, the intractably violent nature of criminal predators, and the unreliability of a rehabilitation-oriented penal establishment and its experts. The decade also produced iconic images of crime and prisoners that continue to circulate even today as the imagined threats underlying most popular crime discourse. One of these images was the prisoner as revolutionary terrorist engaged in an intractable war with the state and its agents. A second was the serial killer, the criminal as psychopathic mastermind driven to horrific violence by irrational desires, capable of killing over and over again. Since the 1970s, these stereotypes, updated with the latest features, have remained the dominant icons in popular culture (true-crime reporting) and scientific criminology, despite the fact that together they account for only a tiny portion of even the most violent subset of criminals.

*   *   *

The new common sense about prisoners of the 1970s replaced a very different narrative that had lasted through most of the post–World War II era. From what historians can tell using media coverage and popular culture, public interest in and sympathy for prisoners was actually approaching a high-water mark in the late 1960s. Although violent crime was already a very visible topic of public concern, other cultural trends, especially the broadening embrace of civil rights values associated with Martin Luther King Jr.'s leadership and the prestige of social science (which was somewhat enthralled with the project of rehabilitative penology), tilted the media landscape at least modestly in favor of the incarcerated. Ironically, on the eve of a tough on crime crackdown, Californians were prepared to see prisoners in a more sympathetic light in 1970 than in 1960 or 1950.

The civil rights movement was an important contributor to this sympathy for prisoners. After all, a disproportionate share of American prisoners then as now were African American and Latino, people systematically deprived of equal rights. Prisons were part of a system of law enforcement that was commonly arbitrary, secretive, and racist.

American social science, which was enjoying a period of prestige at the national level, also contributed to this upgrading of the social worth of prisoners. Most social scientists of the Progressive Era (the 1880s through the 1920s) accepted the categorization of criminals as distinct types whose life patterns could best be understood using the model of pathology borrowed from medicine. By the early 1960s, however, influential scholars were treating crime and delinquency as part of the larger problem of deviance and pathseeking in a posttraditional society that left everyone—but especially youth—personally responsible for forging their future.[15]

To social scientists, prisons were microcosms of society in which individuals struggled to produce meaningful lives within structures of inequality and suppression. The inmate "society" as Gresham Sykes styled it, revealed the power of adaptation, as actors trapped in a forced culture of deprivation created new social institutions to make up for those from which they had been separated.[16] To the sociologists of the 1960s, this spelled bad news for the rehabilitative enterprise, for that was based on the opportunity to rework prisoners more easily by removing them from society. Instead, prisoner society might negate the impact of treatment regimes or even produce deeper criminal commitments. This pessimism about incarceration went along with a great deal of sympathy for the position of the individual prisoner. Whether social science influenced popular culture or simply followed the same narrative trails, we can see much the same attitude in the plots of popular books and films such as Cool Hand Luke (1967), or the British television series The Prisoner (1967–68). These narratives implied that prisoners were protagonists in a battle of the individual against the totalitarian power of the state.

This positive tilt toward prisoners dramatically reversed itself in the 1970s. Two interlinked events at the start of the decade played an outsize role. The violent takeover of part of San Quentin State Prison in California in August 1971 and the uprising in Attica State Prison in New York two weeks later, followed by even more violent reassertions of state authority in both prisons, began the decade with blood and horror. Because these incidents of extraordinary violence took place in the nation's two largest states—which also boasted two of the most progressive, rehabilitation-oriented penal systems—and because California and New York were also centers of the nation's mass media, both events took on national importance. Mainstream media coverage helped define prisoners at a moment of growing anxiety about crime and the capacity of government to respond to it.

The prison rebellions produced a cascade of effects for different audiences. For the minority supporting prisoners in their civil rights struggle, the murderous reprisals confirmed their worst fears about the authoritarian intentions of the prison establishment. For the portion of the general public potentially sympathetic to prisoners but also very alarmed about crime and dependent on biased reporting, the violence on both sides was blamed on the prisoners and became part of a harsher view of criminals. No doubt, the fact that the prison population made visible by these events was predominantly African American and Latino, unlike when social science and popular culture had first framed the story of prisons in the 1940s, must have facilitated the rapid diminution of sympathy and increase of fear. For the far smaller but increasingly politicized force of prison officers, the events represented both the direct threat of an enduring insurgency of prisoners and also the indirect threat of public sympathy for prisoners.

In California, where public interest in and sympathy for prisoners was perhaps the highest in the nation during 1960s and early 1970s, support for the prisoner-rights movement had been growing beyond its traditional strongholds on the left, and might have coalesced into prison and sentencing reform in the course of the decade.[17] However, in the midst of this rise in public attention to prisoners, the turn toward increasingly radical rhetoric and violent action behind bars, greatly magnified by state actors, the media, the prison officers' union, produced an enduring public image of prisoners as revolutionary terrorists engaged in an unending struggle with both prison and society—an image that came ultimately to weaken the prisoner-rights movement.[18]

Prisoners came to be identified with one man, a brilliant, charismatic African American prisoner, political theorist, and revolutionary, George Jackson. While Jackson's story is less well known outside California, it's worth reviewing, because it set the terms of the state's prison-expansion policy in the 1980s and provided an icon of the convict-as-revolutionary-terrorist that would reset the national common sense about prisons and prisoners. Jackson was sent to prison in 1960 on what was expected to be a sentence of a year or less, but he had served more than a decade when he died in 1971, a result of California's indeterminate sentencing law that allowed the state to imprison most felons until rehabilitated. Jackson became educated in prison and ultimately rose to be a leader of black prisoners and the national Black Panther Party. He became a major link between the prisoners' movement inside and the black nationalist and radical political movements. On the outside, Jackson's book *Soledad Brother: The Prison Letters of George Jackson*, received glowing reviews and became a bestseller. For the many impressed and inspired by George Jackson as a writer and political theorist, Jackson's treatment revealed a legal system that held its prisoners under threat of permanent incarceration no matter the gravity of the felony,[19] demonstrating its totalitarianism and its racism. The book's depiction of arbitrary racist rule inside California prisons was resonant with the emerging mainstream view and carried his message and fame well beyond his base in the radical left.

Inside, Jackson was accused by prison authorities of leading a campaign of retaliatory violence against prison officers and white prisoners. Facing first-degree-murder charges that would add the possibility of a death sentence to the life sentence he was already serving, Jackson was placed, along with a number of his associates, in the special disciplinary unit of San Quentin prison. Foreshadowing today's supermax prisons, the Adjustment Center at San Quentin featured solitary confinement and exclusion from prison programs and work assignments. On August 21, 1971, in events that have never been fully explained, Jackson obtained a gun and set about freeing prisoners and taking officers hostage inside the Adjustment Center. The following description comes from one of the many appeals of Johnny Spain, Jackson's trusted associate who, unlike Jackson, survived the takeover and became the only prisoner convicted of the killings there:

> On August 21, 1971, there was an outburst of deadly violence at the Adjustment Center. George Jackson, also a member of the Black Panther Party, returned to the Adjustment Center after meeting with his lawyer, Stephen Bingham. When guards found a bullet clip on Jackson, Jackson removed a gun from under his wig and forced one of the guards present to open the cells of other prisoners. Many of the prisoners, including Spain, emerged from their cells. There was testimony that Spain played a role in binding guards and placing them in the cells where they subsequently were assaulted. He was seen approaching the guards with an earphone cord in his hands. The cord was of the type used to bind the guards. There also was testimony that at one point he held Jackson's gun, which was used to murder two of the guards.

When an alarm was sounded, Jackson and Spain fled from the Adjustment Center, Jackson with a gun in his hand and Spain with some keys. Jackson was shot by guards and was killed instantly. Spain dove into some bushes where he was found hiding. When order was restored the aftermath of the violence was revealed: one officer had bled to death from a neck wound; two had been shot to death in the head; three others had their throats slashed, but survived; and two prisoners died of similar wounds. The Director of Corrections called the incident the worst in her eight years as Director.[20]

Whatever Jackson's political writing and prison organizing might have led to if he had lived, his death and the fact that both admirers and enemies often played up his violent legacy produced one of the defining images of the prisoner as threat to society. Historian Eric Cummins summarizes Jackson's posthumous career:

The real George Jackson quickly became unimportant anyway. For those who had appropriated his myth as their own, for the [violent revolutionary factions] BGF [Black Guerrilla Family] and the SLA [Symbionese Liberation Army], Jackson was now the Dragon, who had passed on to them the foco [Spanish for "focus"] tactic, key to the future struggle. For the California Correctional Officers Association and other groups on the Right, on the contrary, Jackson's memory would become a rallying cry for a conservative backlash against further prison reform.[21]

Jackson's death galvanized California's correctional bureaucracy and reshaped its thinking for a generation. But the broader national common sense about prisons might have survived his dramatic death had its violent imagery not been reproduced in even more spectacular and iconic ways less than a month later at a prison in another large and media-centered state, Attica State Prison in New York.

At Attica, a well-organized alliance of prisoners of all races had been steadily gaining strength and public interest for their campaign against poor conditions, especially at medical facilities, in New York prisons. Moved by news of Jackson's death and by abusive actions of prison officers, prisoners took over the prison on September 9, 1971, taking thirty-three prison officers hostage and presenting authorities with a list of demands to be met before they would agree to restore normal authority in the prison. Most of these demands were for basic improvements in prison conditions, and accounts suggest that the authorities were close to agreeing to virtually all of them except the demand for amnesty for the rebellion leaders. But with great national public attention on the prison, Governor Nelson Rockefeller made the decision to cut off negotiations and ordered a violent retaking of the prison. Under cover of a barrage of tear gas, more than six hundred prison officers and state police officers, many of them armed with personal weapons, retook the prison, killing twenty-nine prisoners and eleven of the hostages in an unrelenting hail of bullets.

The unnecessary and lethal retaking of the prison might have backfired on the governor and vindicated the prisoners, who were represented by articulate and respected journalists and lawyers. But as historian Heather Thompson documents, state officials decided to lie.

Officials stood outside of Attica after the assault, looked straight into the TV cameras, and stated that the hostages had each died because inmates had slit their throats. Worse, they said, one guard had actually been castrated and the inmate who did it shoved the guard's testicles into his own mouth. . . .

Most tragically, this "official" version of what had gone so wrong at Attica is what made the front page of hundreds of newspapers across the country—from the esteemed *New York Times* to the *Los Angeles Times*, and to many a small town paper as well. And any sympathy for the plight of America's incarcerated, any sense that they needed a greater voice in society or needed advocates among the nation's voting population, began to evaporate.[22]

No state official was ever charged with a crime for the atrocity. Although the official story was swiftly discredited in the elite media, it was seldom corrected in the mass media, and Attica became a defining event for prisons for the next generation. Between the death of George Jackson and the retaking of Attica, a new common sense about prisoners took shape. Even though it was the state that killed the Attica hostages, the tale of sadistic revolutionary prisoners mobilized correctional officers behind calls for harsher punishment. Tensions mounted on both sides. Assaults on staff, generally rare in California before the late 1960s, began to grow rapidly, from thirty-two in 1969 to eighty-four in 1973. While the violence soon died down, the perception by California prison officers that they faced an unending war with prisoners was firmly established and motivated support for a union organizing effort based on identification with crime victims rather than with other state workers, such as teachers or nurses.[23]

Of course, images alone do not forge policies. In New York, California, and everywhere in between, the next two decades would see a successful coalition of police, prison officers, politicians, and pundits demand and receive a panoply of tough new laws requiring longer prison sentences, harsher prison conditions, more executions, and new powers and benefits for law enforcement.[24] Although the prisoner uprisings ended almost as quickly as they began, the largely false image of the prisoner as revolutionary terrorist replaced the image of the prisoner as a kind of hapless everyman, guilty of his crimes perhaps, but an underdog against the grinding dehumanization of prison and the injustice of society outside. This image dated back to the Big House movies of the 1930s but would not be evoked again until, at the height of mass incarceration, 1994's *Shawshank Redemption* reached back into the past to depict prisoners sympathetically.

This changing narrative went along with a shift in the racial makeup of the prison population.[25] The older image of prisoners, invariably white, was often the subject of implicit sympathy. Whatever real threat their criminal career had posed was suspended if not ended by the fact of their imprisonment. The new image represented the prisoner as a relentless lethal threat not just to frontline prison officers but to ordinary citizens in their homes. The new iconic prisoner, frequently black or brown, was an unchangeable menace barely contained by the prison. This image facilitated the message of the emerging coalition in support of mass incarceration. It hung like an albatross around the neck of a generation of liberal groups and celebrities who had championed prisoners' rights in the 1960s but who largely subsided from the debate after the 1970s.

* * *

The 1970s also witnessed the rise of powerful new images of violent crime outside prison, with strong implications for criminal justice, as several monstrous serial killers helped reshape our common sense about crime prevention. California was again the epicenter, with the most numerous and best-publicized set of serial killing episodes in the country. Between 1969 and 1979, nearly a score of serial killing episodes with well over 150 confirmed victims took place in California. As a criminological phenomenon, serial killing followed much the same historical pattern as violence generally, with reported increases in the 1960s through the 1980s and a decline after the early 1990s.[26] Nor was California actually exposed to a disproportionate share of serial killers. But the state's exaggerated fears and hopes about itself, along with its concentration of media resources, assured that its experiences with this most sensational of crimes would scar public consciousness there even as the number of new incidents declined.

One highly visible result was a permanent place for the serial killer in popular culture—in "slasher films," including *Friday the 13th, Halloween*, and *Nightmare on Elm Street*, as well as in mainstream movies, such as *The Silence of the Lambs*.[27] But although citizens would pay money to be stimulated by safe exposure to predators in films, in real life the effect was a general hardening in attitudes toward criminals and prisoners. Rehabilitation was not an option for serial killers, who could use the therapeutic presumptions of treatment to manipulate their way to freedom. The serial killer was a meme for the new common sense about criminals generally, i.e., that they *all* were unchanging in their criminality but prolix and flexible in their predatory choices.

The national debate about the death penalty was one area of policy in which the serial killer (along with the convict-revolutionary) instantly played a role. The Supreme Court's 1972 *Furman v. Georgia* decision, striking down all of the nation's death-penalty statutes (although leaving the door open to a "reformed" capital-sentencing process) occurred as the increase in serial homicides, begun in the early 1960s, continued into its second decade. Indeed, Charles Manson and his cohorts had been sentenced to death only a year or so before California's Supreme Court anticipated *Furman* by several months and struck down the state's death penalty statute as violating the U.S. Constitution.[28] Many people opposed the death penalty because of concerns about racism and judicial fallibility, but famous serial killers such as Manson provided resonant examples of criminals whom even they could support executing.[29] As a result of the *Furman* decision, all prisoners on death row in the United States had their sentences reset to whatever the legal alternative was to the death penalty. Because parole laws around the country were often quite lenient in allowing early release, including for those with life sentences, former death row inmates were eligible for parole in the relatively near future. In California, first-degree murderers would be eligible for parole after seven years, following *Furman*, which meant that Manson family members came up for parole before the end of the decade (though they would be denied repeatedly for decades to come). Serial killers also shaped public attitudes toward those who commit far less serious crimes, including burglary, credit-card theft, and small-scale drug trafficking; the mythology that serial killers helped create suggested that, far from being reassuring, low-level crimes may indicate a predator-to-be.

The market for true-crime books and television shows about serial killers is still lively. As profilers like to remind us, the real serial killer is strikingly older, whiter, and more middle-class than the "usual suspects" in violent-crime narratives. This made the serial killer a fitting complement to the usually dark-skinned convict-revolutionaries. As an iconic image, the serial killer brings the threat of murder into spaces imagined as white, middle-class, and safe. The serial killer evaded all the environmental protections that middle-class citizens could access by moving away from city centers to middle-class white (or increasingly Asian) suburban neighborhoods accessible only by car. Often white and middle-class themselves, serial killers invaded nice houses and neighborhoods, attacked people in their nonurban recreational settings, or perhaps most terrifyingly of all found them at vulnerable points on the ubiquitous California freeways that were the inescapable public place of the new suburban residential lifestyle.

The serial-killer threat was a powerful exhibit for a new common sense about crime prevention. It taught citizens a number of "lessons" that went something like this: Even apparently normal people are capable of rapid descent into lethal violence precipitated by the loss of moral boundaries of the self, especially when facilitated by powerful psychotropic drugs. No easily observable sociological factors can adequately predict this kind of aberrational turn, but it almost always goes along with a general pattern of lawbreaking. Once a person has abandoned moral boundaries, it was assumed, the minor desires of the self are as likely to lead to crimes as the most heinous and major. Such a person will not always have a criminal record, for police and the courts are far from perfect. Therefore the legal system should incapacitate the perpetrators of all crimes when they are first arrested, against the possibility that they are on a descent that will lead to lethal violence. Many California serial killers had been confined by the state before, in youth prisons, state mental hospitals, or adult prisons, and quite a few in all three. Thus along with the terrifying iconic image of the serial killer as a master criminal, the story line that emerged was of a dull-witted or naive state bureaucracy that kept blowing chances to protect Californians from the worst kinds of violent criminals.

California's revolutionary prisoners and serial killers of the 1970s, along with the political and media complexes drawn to each, helped reshape the common sense about prisons, prisoners, and crime prevention in two senses. First, a long-standing conception of prisoners as hapless, changeable underdogs was replaced by an image of the monster, a creature of unrelenting, unmotivated predatory violence. Second, the broad range of twentieth-century penal measures in response to felony crime, including supervision in the community,[30] was dramatically reduced, so that physical isolation in security-oriented prisons came to be the only trusted form of state crime control. While the era of mass incarceration would see a vast new population of marginal offenders swept into prisons, the rare but iconic prisoners—revolutionaries and serial killers, mostly of a bygone era—would form the template around which the new security regime was constructed.

* * *

In our federal system, states have broad discretion to determine the purposes of prison, and the courts defer greatly to those rationales in ruling on the constitutionality of any challenged practices. In the 1970s and 1980s, courts cited the prevailing commitment to rehabilitation in defining nonrehabilitative practices that betrayed that premise as unconstitutional.[31] More recently, by contrast, the Supreme Court has cited California's preference for incapacitation and deterrence in upholding punitive practices such as three-strikes laws.[32]

As recently as the early 1970s, treatment or rehabilitation was almost universally embraced as the modern rationale for imprisonment. While rehabilitation and its correlate institutions, such as parole, were always viewed skeptically by the general public and the media, these approaches were widely embraced by judges, lawyers, and politicians through the late 1960s.[33]

Beginning in the 1970s, however, many influential legal theorists began openly to criticize rehabilitation, not on the grounds that it was insufficiently punitive (most were liberals not particularly interested in more punishment) but on the grounds that, by treating the prisoner as an object to be "fixed," rehabilitative penology denied prisoners their "dignity," understood largely as "autonomy." This stance was part of a legal understanding of "human dignity," a concept being revitalized in the public law of many democracies in response to the atrocities of World War II, reflected in documents including the Universal Declaration of Human Rights, which was circulated in 1948.

In the 1970s, this dignity movement reached sentencing law. Drawing on the eighteenth-century philosopher Immanuel Kant's influential account of punishment as a moral obligation, many legal academics and philosophers in this first wave of "dignity thinking" asserted that using human beings, even felons, as a means to advance social goals, such as crime prevention, violated their dignity, and that only the goal of just punishment for wrongdoing truly respects the autonomy of the prisoner as a person equal in dignity to any other. While Kant's preference for punishment as a moral good was actually embedded in his complex (and to us all but incomprehensible) metaphysical commitments, the "just deserts" advocates of the 1970s shared neither those metaphysics nor his commitment to suffering. Instead, they argued for short, determinate sentences proportionate to the severity of the crime.[34] For many, a return to a modest retributivism was a way to limit the arbitrary power of the state and assure equality to all prisoners regardless of race.

In retrospect, the prison debates of the 1970s appear strangely irrelevant. Proponents of deterrence, rehabilitation, and retribution engaged in furious argument in the pages of law reviews but made little effort to engage the public or address the looming issue of fear of crime. None of these elites in the mid-1970s advocated the creation of a vastly larger prison population, nor did they argue for construction of an archipelago of new prisons with capacity exceeding by many times the number of prisoners then held. The penal rationale of incapacitation, the belief that prison prevents crimes that would occur if prisoners were free, was rarely part of the discussion.

In their pioneering study of the rise of incapacitation as a penal rationale, Franklin Zimring and Gordon Hawkins note the rather surprising way in which incapacitation had come to dominate policy despite a near absence of criminological writing on the subject.[35] Puzzled by its stealth success, Zimring and Hawkins ascribe incapacitation's ascendance to a process of elimination, "as scholarly and public debate about the other functions of imprisonment undermined faith in prison rehabilitation as an effective process and in deterrence as a basis for making fine-tuned allocations of imprisonment resources."[36]

This may explain how elites made their peace with total incapacitation and the large prison populations it would require, but it does not explain the strength of California's political commitment to an extreme version of this strategy. By the end of the 1970s, key politicians supported expanding the prison population.[37] Incapacitation gave supporters of prison expansion a rationale with expert legitimacy (if not enthusiasm) and a strong emotional appeal to a populace haunted by the 1970s crime icons.

The idea that prison, by separating dedicated criminals from vulnerable potential victims, is both necessary and sufficient to repress the worst kinds of crime is at least a plausible rational strategy if your criminal class is made up of potential serial killers and/or committed revolutionary convicts (or today's terrorists at Guantánamo). With the new iconic images of violence threatening citizens wherever they lived, any reduction in the level of imprisonment would be a direct reduction in the security of people in their homes.

Incapacitation also fit well with the general sense of pessimism about the capacity of government to change individual behavior; the belief that most criminals are irredeemable became something of a consensus among criminologists and other social scientists in the 1970s, something both liberals and conservatives agreed on. As Zimring and Hawkins cogently observe, incapacitation relies on

> the implicit assumption that criminal offenders are intractable and insusceptible to change. . . . Indeed an image of the criminal offender as intractable was very much in fashion in the United States by the 1990s. Thus, the attack on rehabilitation encouraged a view of criminal offenders that made incapacitation appear to be a singularly suitable policy goal for prisons.[38]

Incapacitation also fit with a new common sense about crime prevention, in which the once distinct categories of criminals and prisoners had collapsed together. In the public imagination, the image of the vulnerable individual in the grip of the prison regime had given way to the unfathomable criminal threat in custody.

This collapse of categories is integral to one of the most consequential features of California's total-incapacitation approach, the preference for general rather than selective incapacitation. Incapacitation achieves its crime-prevention effect by separating active offenders from society. For much of the twentieth century, U.S. prison systems claimed to be selective in their incapacitation. Judicious use of incapacitation was considered the counterbalance to rehabilitation's promise to treat and release most offenders, paroling those with good prospects for going straight and imposing long prison sentences on the incorrigible. In one way or another, selective incapacitation relies on expertise, either in clinical form as appraisal of a dense record or in actuarial form as analysis of risk factors. By contrast, California after the 1970s eschewed expertise of any sort, embracing a general incapacitation of all felons even as legislators continually added to the list of available felonies.

By the early 1980s, an extreme version of general incapacitation, with deterrence and justice (retribution) as minor themes, prevailed in California not only in both major political parties but also to a large extent among both elites and the general public. No combination of declining crime rates or rising fiscal costs could overcome the impulse to imprison. Abandoning rehabilitation was important, but the additional emphasis on general incapacitation made California's extreme prison-population growth and the humanitarian crisis of its prisons all but inevitable.[39]

Although the shift to general incapacitation helps explain the manyfold expansion of the captive population (the quantitative story), it alone however cannot account for California's qualitative regression in the treatment of prisoners. Almost two decades after Zimring and Hawkins pondered the triumph of incapacitation, it is clear that California has adopted a version so extreme as to be historically unique—*total* incapacitation. As a penal rationale, incapacitation is popular all over the world, including western Europe, where it goes along with a commitment to rehabilitative prisons and a small imprisonment rate. Most incapacitation policies include some form of restraint, some ability to define limits, and lines drawn by recognition of and respect for our shared humanity. California, bedeviled by the monstrous fears of the 1970s, abandoned almost all of those restraints, resulting in a literally totalitarian project with little precedent in America's modern era. While the varieties of incapacitation logic that have influenced the expansion of imprisonment across the country are generally less virulent than California's strain, its model of total incapacitation reveals features that have driven that growth beyond rational bounds in almost every state over the past forty years.

The essential elements of this totalitarian brand of incapacitation distinguish it from its more democratic cousins. First, total incapacitation defines custody in a prison as the only meaningful incapacitation. It reflects a fundamental mistrust of correctionalism as practiced in California and elsewhere throughout the twentieth century. It rejects less drastic first resorts, including supervision and surveillance in the community, sometimes combined with a shorter term of custody served in a local jail, occupational restrictions, reporting requirements, and even pharmacological treatments.

Second, under total incapacitation preventive control has gone from being a reason for sending someone to prison to being a way of operating prisons. Historically, the walls achieved incapacitation, while the prison's internal regime was arranged for other goals that states believed would turn prisoners away from crime, including penitence, discipline, labor, education, and later therapy. In California in the era of total incapacitation, prisons became all about incapacitation internally; security and control replaced education, labor, and treatment almost completely.

Third, as noted above, American imprisonment was historically selective, imposed on those whose repeated or serious crimes indicated a high level of danger to public safety. Total incapacitation is indiscriminate. Whole categories of people are incapacitated regardless of the risk they pose to the community.[40]

Fourth, total incapacitation recognizes no prospect of change in the criminal risk posed by offenders throughout their lives. Ideally, in this view, all punishment for all crimes would be life imprisonment, thereby eliminating the individual crime risk entirely. Any actual limitations on punishment arise not from an assessment of risk but rather because the current law is not yet severe enough (although for a long time its trend was only toward longer terms) or because life sentences are simply too expensive for everyone. European (and bygone American) incapacitation policies recognize that maturation reduces criminal risk. The danger posed by a twenty-five-year-old is seldom the same as that posed by a forty-five-year-old. This recognition favors mechanisms including parole and executive clemency, which can permit review of sentences even years later. American states, by contrast, have embraced policies that make no such distinctions but instead make revision difficult and politically costly.

No one could really defend the idea that a criminal risk continues no matter the personal circumstances of a prisoner (for example, if he was paralyzed) or that every offender, no matter how low level his crimes, could be on the way to becoming a serial killer. Yet our penal practices in California took these absurdities as core assumptions, beginning in the 1980s. From the mid-1980s to 2004, California built twenty-two entirely new prisons, many of them massive. Those years also witnessed the parallel enactment by California's legislature of harsh new sentencing laws intended to overfill them. Such laws—routine extensions of statutory terms and special sentence-enhancement measures triggered by high-publicity crimes, such as California's notoriously extreme three-strikes law [41]—have drawn on a way of imagining criminals and prisoners that took shape and became enshrined in the 1970s.

That historical mind-set explains why a political solution to mass incarceration has been so hard to achieve. Excesses in most areas of public policy are checked by the eager resistance of political forces that roughly balance forces on the other side. But that kind of political competition has not happened with respect to incarceration. By the end of the 1970s, the new common sense about crime, prisons, and prisoners had settled over the entire spectrum of politics in California and many other states. Left and right continued to field competing views about criminal justice, but only within the parameters of general incapacitation.

As Zimring and Hawkins predicted in the mid-1990s, the logic of incapacitation creates a perilous trap for anyone who would recommend changes in law that might result in fewer people being sent to state prison or shorter terms. Such a person would appear to choose hope about the future behavior of criminal offenders over fears for the harms that their victims have suffered and might suffer. Indeed, the logic of incapacitation virtually assured that no amount of prison growth could drain the reservoir of fear on which support for mass incarceration now floated.

Efforts at rehabilitation rest on the belief that many if not most prisoners actually can be rehabilitated. If even a few commit new crimes after they are released, that belief is quickly put under extreme stress. Not so with total incapacitation. If the overall goal of imprisonment is only to reduce the risk posed by known offenders to innocent members of the public, the fact that some former prisoners commit new crimes simply confirms that it would have been better to have kept them all locked up even longer.[42] Incapacitation enjoys a kind of axiomatic success that is immune to empirical evidence. As Zimring and Hawkins write, "Just as locking up more offenders *must* reduce criminal activity by some amount, releasing large numbers of offenders or allowing them to remain outside prison *must* produce some increase in the number of crimes experienced in the community that receives [or keeps] them."[43]

The total-incapacitation mind-set locked California into an unsustainable situation in which the state's prison population, no matter how huge, could *never* provide enough protection against crime to satisfy the political demand for security, while any effort to redirect people away from prison or release them early was viewed as an inevitable threat to public safety. This produced a deadlock in which, despite widespread recognition of the system's problems, there has been no political will to solve them. It is in the face of this paralysis that the courts have come to play such a crucial role.

In the mid-1990s, Zimring and Hawkins presciently noted two factors that could halt the growth of prisons. The first of these is fixed limits on prison space. As Zimring and Hawkins observe,

> Incapacitation claims are only open ended if the extent of the custodial facilities available can vary freely. If there are externally imposed limits on the scale and growth of imprisonment, incapacitation as a purpose may influence how cell space is utilized but cannot determine how much of it is available.[44]

For a long time it seemed as if this limit would not be reached in California. A number of economic and political factors aligned to support expanding the physical space of imprisonment in California in the 1980s and 1990s.[45] These forces were largely independent of the criminal justice imperatives for incapacitation; they included surpluses of finance capital, of farmland, and the existence of a set of young men with little education and little apparent value to the economy. As that group of exploitable opportunities fell apart in the late 1990s, the expansion of prison space stopped altogether.

Although prison building stalled, the policy of mass incarceration was still firmly entrenched among the county-level officials, prosecutors, judges, and even defense lawyers, who together determine which of those convicted of felonies are sent to prison. The predictable result was gross overcrowding that reached the crisis point at the start of the new century. Limits on the stock of prison cells might have sets limits on the growth of incarceration in California but did not. California was apparently willing to tolerate grossly overcrowded prisons. It would take something more than physical limits.

The second factor that Zimring and Hawkins point to as having the potential to mitigate the appeal of incapacitation was a change in the basic pessimism about the ability of non-prison measures to prevent crime:

An emphasis on incapacitation is particularly suited to periods of pessimism about the efficacy of government programs and the capacity of individuals to undergo positive change. It is in this context that we have referred to incapacitation as a penal purpose of last resort. Historical evidence demonstrates that attitudes regarding both the malleability of offenders and the capacity of government programs to achieve constructive results are cyclical. . . . Any increase in public confidence about the prospect of using a wider variety of crime control strategies is likely to reduce the relative emphasis on incapacitation from its recent levels in criminal justice administration.[46]

The remarkable crime decline throughout the United States since the early 1990s has created the conditions for a renewed debate about how government can address crime. Some have continued to argue that mass incarceration produced the decline, so no change is necessary or desirable.[47] Close study of the crime decline, however, provides little reason to believe that current rates must be maintained to keep crime low.[48] Those states that have reduced crime the most are not the most enthusiastic jailers. Instead, other mechanisms, especially innovative police practices, seem more relevant. As Zimring and Hawkins predicted, an increased belief in the ability of government to control crime has led to a reconsideration of total incapacitation, by the public and by courts.

If there is an exit from the iron cage of total incapacitation and mass incarceration left by the fear years of the 1970s, it will require institutions that can enforce limits to prison population growth while encouraging optimism about the capacity of alternative measures to address crime threats to the community. Historically for the United States, that institution has been the federal courts, which have acted as a vehicle for those without the political clout necessary to attack entrenched state practices such as segregation and coercive hospitalization without treatment of people with mental illness. But for much of the time mass incarceration policies have been in place, the federal courts have responded to claims of mistreatment by California prisoners without significantly constraining the overall drift toward inhumane conditions in prisons. In California's case, the intervention would finally come in the form of a remarkable series of civil rights suits that would frame the inhumanity of California's prisons in terms of the mental and physical suffering of the state's many chronically ill prisoners.

2

The House of Fear

Dignity and Risk in Madrid v. Gomez

Mass imprisonment is usually thought of in terms of scale, but it comes with a distinctive approach to the content or quality of imprisonment, which is characterized by emptiness and a lack of ambition to reform or extract penance from its inmates, turning prisons into mere human warehouses aimed at nothing more than custody. No practice epitomizes this feature more than the supermax-style prison, which has been adopted widely since first being introduced by Arizona in 1982.[1] Forty-four out of fifty states, the federal government, and of course the military (for its war on terror) now operate supermax prisons. Supermax imprisonment has grown much faster than imprisonment in general.[2] Supermax cells are designed to minimize the risk of violence by allowing a prisoner's daily needs to be met with virtually no direct contact with other prisoners or prison officers. Typically, supermax prisoners remain in their cells for twenty-three hours a day, taking all their meals there and leaving their cells only for one hour for exercise or showering.

Although California was not the first state to adopt supermax prisons, its massive Pelican Bay Security Housing Unit (SHU) would become the locus of the leading national challenge to the constitutionality of the practice, *Madrid v. Gomez*.[3] Judge Thelton Henderson's opinion, based on one of the most thorough judicial investigations ever undertaken of a prison regime, belongs among the most significant modern narratives of prison conditions, comparable in its critical gaze to the much earlier observations of prison by Alexis de Tocqueville, Charles Dickens, and John Howard.[4] The case exposed in shocking detail the extremes of mental deterioration in prisoners and of abusive violence by prison officers. Perhaps most important, the case was the first to correctly identify the constitutional significance of mass incarceration's failure to reckon with the biological and psychological consequences of its practices and the consequent threat to human dignity. This understanding helped to revitalize the constitutional significance of dignity for the Eighth Amendment's prohibition on cruel and unusual punishment.

Legally, the *Madrid* opinion offered a mix of victories and defeats for both the plaintiff prisoners and the state defendants. The court found that key aspects of the operation of the Security Housing Unit—its violent control tactics and lack of mental health care—violated the Eighth Amendment's ban of cruel and unusual punishment. In and of itself, however, incarceration in the Security Housing Unit was found to be *not* cruel and unusual, but the court identified one group of prisoners—those with an existing mental illness—for whom such punishment was unquestionably cruel and unusual. Placing such mentally ill prisoners in the SHU was, as Judge Henderson unforgettably (and presciently) puts it "the mental equivalent of putting an asthmatic in a place with little air to breathe."[5] Judge Henderson also considers whether the correction department's sweeping discretion to assign prisoners to the Security Housing Unit for any length of time within their legal prison sentence provided sufficient due process as required by the Fourteenth

Amendment's ban on depriving people of liberty "without due process of law."

In his *Madrid* opinion, Judge Henderson describes in detail the Security Housing Unit at Pelican Bay:

Each cell is 80 square feet and comes equipped with two built-in bunks and a toilet-sink unit. Cell doors are made of heavy gauge perforated metal; this design prevents objects from being thrown through the door but also significantly blocks vision and light. A skylight in each pod does allow some natural light to enter the tier area adjacent to the cells; however, cells are primarily lit with a fluorescent light that can be operated by the inmate. Each cell block is supervised and guarded by a separate control station which is staffed by armed correctional officers and separated from the pods by an electronically controlled metal gate. The officers also electronically control the opening and closing of the cell doors.

Patterned after a "Special Management Unit" in Florence, Arizona (albeit with some modifications), the SHU interior is designed to reduce visual stimulation. The cellblocks are marked throughout by a dull sameness in design and color. The cells are windowless; the walls are white concrete. When inside the cell, all one can see through the perforated metal door is another white wall.

A small exercise pen with cement floors and walls is attached to the end of each pod. Because the walls are 20 feet high, they preclude any view of the outside world. The top of the pen is covered partly by a screen and partly by a plastic rain cover, thus providing access to some fresh air. However, given their cell-like design and physical attachment to the pod itself, the pens are more suggestive of satellite cells than areas for exercise or recreation.

The overall effect of the SHU is one of stark sterility and unremitting monotony. Inmates can spend years without ever seeing any aspect of the outside world except for a small patch of sky. One inmate fairly described the SHU as being "like a space capsule where one is shot into space and left in isolation."

The supermax should not be understood as a solution to a technical problem. Rather, California's SHU prisons operate to assuage the fears that produced mass incarceration in the first place. Indeed, Pelican Bay SHU, the largest of five supermax units in California today and the only one purposely built for that function, is a working monument to the social agreement made in the 1970s to incapacitate a group defined as a monolithic and permanently dangerous class.

*   *   *

California was not the first jurisdiction to develop supermax prisons; Arizona opened the first state supermax prison in 1987, named Special Management Unit I, in Florence.[6] But California was the first state to turn supermax into a permanent strategy for managing the general prison population, with consequences for the basic decency of prisons that we will be considering for much of the rest of this book.

The story of California's supermax Pelican Bay Security Housing Unit and the *Madrid* litigation begins nearly twenty years earlier, in the violence that erupted at San Quentin State Prison on August 21, 1971, when George Jackson and his compatriots took over the Adjustment Center, and a new narrative about prisoners was solidified.[7] California's political establishment had not yet committed itself to mass incarceration, but the future brutality of total incapacitation had already been determined. The first prisoners to experience this new style of incarceration in California were the survivors of the Adjustment Center takeover: the San Quentin Six, including Johnny Spain, the named plaintiff in *Spain v. Procunier* and the man whom prison officials believed had been George Jackson's second in command during the takeover.[8] Litigation over the treatment of the San Quentix Six would last for years. A decade later, when California authorized a wave of new prison construction and gave administrators a free hand to determine what kind of units to build, they chose to include two supersized supermax units. When criminologist and legal scholar Keramet Reiter asked the planners of this system why they chose to invest so heavily in this new and controversial type of prison, they cited the Adjustment Center takeover and other assaults on officers in 1971:

> High-level administrators, who were managing California's prisons in the 1980s, mentioned this event in three different interviews, remembering the exact date, describing in graphic detail how the "officers were cut ear-to-ear," and counting the unusually high number of correctional officers who had died throughout California prisons in 1971 (eleven).[9]

It is perhaps the origin of this strategy as a response to crisis levels of violence that helps explain two other distinctive features of California's supermax regime in addition to scale. First, California's SHU units were fitted with bunk beds for routine double-celling. Second, California extended supermax placement from short-term disciplinary treatment to indefinite isolation. Recent criticism of supermax has emphasized the mental issues caused or worsened by solitary confinement, which was associated with madness even in the nineteenth century. From this perspective, California's practice of regular double-celling might seem a humane gesture, lessening the isolation. But combined with the absence of work, education, or treatment programs, the double-celling has been documented to make prisoners' sense of claustrophobia, stress, physical discomfort, and lack of privacy worse, not better. In any event, it is clear that the desire to maximize capacity, not any concern for prisoners, determined the use of double-celling, and this is the most salient point.[10] California went into its supermax program *anticipating* that it would be a permanent, large-scale enterprise, not an exceptional remedy for the most violent and incorrigible criminals. And California adopted another distinctive practice: use of supermax as a long-term housing option for prisoners presumed to be leaders in prison gangs.[11]

Supermax prisons represent only a small portion of the total number of new prisons California constructed during the era of mass incarceration. Nevertheless, they have helped legitimize mass incarceration. In supermax, the popular mandate to incapacitate on an industrial scale meets the prison bureaucracy's assumptions that the danger posed by prisoners is only weakly related to the particular crime they have been imprisoned for and that potentially all inmates are dangerous. Although the supermax prison was never put before the public as a choice in California or anywhere else, its subsequent public fame and the state's strong defense of the practice to this day testify to its importance as an anchor of mass incarceration's legitimacy.

The promise of mass incarceration as stated in the *Spain* formula—to keep "dangerous men, secure, in humane conditions"—is also the core promise of supermax. The existence in California of two one-thousand-cell SHU prisons testifies in steel and concrete to the scale of the threat California's prison managers believed they faced. Designed for isolation, supermax is meant to hold the most dangerous men without risk to staff or other prisoners and without the heavy physical restraints that courts had held might violate the Eighth Amendment, not coincidentally in *Spain v. Procunier* itself.[12] The result is a penal form remarkably immune to its own fail-

ure, because it floats on tides of emotion between politicians
and the public. The violence produced by the supermax only
serves to reaffirm its necessity.

* * *

It is noteworthy that Judge Henderson's opinion in the *Madrid*
decision begins by quoting from *Spain*, acknowledging the
"unenviable task" of prison managers and noting that the mental illnesses afflicting many of those in the SHU makes that
task even harder:

> As the Ninth Circuit has previously said, prison officials
> have the "unenviable task of keeping dangerous men in safe
> custody under humane conditions." *Spain v. Procunier*, 600
> F.2d 189, 193 (9th Cir. 1979). In a place like the SHU, which
> houses some of the most anti-social and violence-prone pris-
> oners in the system—including those who suffer from men-
> tal illness—the task is that much more difficult.

Henderson acknowledges that the supermax prison stands
at the pinnacle of legitimacy claims for all prisons—ostensibly
designed to hold the most dangerous in the most secure and
most humane conditions possible. However, the facts uncov-
ered in the trial of the Pelican Bay SHU disproved every part of
that trinity of assumptions.[13]

Judge Henderson in *Madrid* largely accepts the state's understanding that supermax prisons were designed to hold men
as explosively violent as George Jackson (or at least his legend)
but argues that therefore prison officials have every incentive
to be selective in assignments to the SHU:

> The SHU has gained a well-deserved reputation as a place
> which, by design, imposes conditions far harsher than those
> anywhere else in the California prison system. The roughly

1,000–1,500 inmates confined in the SHU remain isolated in windowless cells for 22 and ½ hours each day, and are denied access to prison work programs and group exercise yards. Assignment to the SHU is not based on the inmate's underlying offense; rather, SHU cells are reserved for those inmates in the California prison system who become affiliated with a prison gang or commit serious disciplinary infractions once in prison. They represent, according to a phrase coined by defendants, "the worst of the worst."[14]

Much turns on the characterization of SHU prisoners as "the worst of the worst," a term the judge intentionally left in quotes. Who, in fact, was the SHU designed for and who has been held there? Thanks to the research of Keramet Reiter cited above, we know that California's convict revolutionaries of the early 1970s were very much on the minds of state prison planners, even though most of the original participants in the Adjustment Center takeover were no longer a threat and some were altogether out of custody when the Pelican Bay SHU opened in 1989.[15] Even at its maximum, this category of prisoners was far too small to fill even a few pods, let alone two supersize supermaxes.

While California's prison bureaucracy was motivated to create supermax prisons by George Jackson in the 1970s, they got their public justification from serial killers in the 1980s. Most serial killers take advantage of vulnerable victims by simple deception (picking up hitchhikers, luring children with candy, and so on), but in popular mythology, they quickly become uncannily resourceful geniuses. The 1991 thriller *The Silence of the Lambs* portrays a predatory villain so malevolent and ingenious that even his jailers need special technological help to keep themselves and the public safe. California had a number of incarcerated serial killers by the time the SHU opened, including iconic serial killer Charles Manson (who was housed in California's Corcoran State Prison SHU for a period). In fact, most serial killers in California were housed elsewhere, either on death row or in less secure units, but the image of the serial killer remains so potent a justication for the SHU that in the summer of 2013, activists supporting a hunger strike within the SHU had to deny that there were currently any serial killers held in the facilities on strike.[16]

Neither convict-revolutionaries nor serial killers are nearly numerous enough to fill the vast supermax prisons California built. Instead, California has relied heavily on another category: identified gang members, who now make up an estimated two thirds of supermax inmates nationwide.[17] California's prison gangs are far larger and more influential over the daily lives of all prisoners than their counterparts in other states.[18] Associated with acts of violence both in and out of prisons and tied to a presumption of permanent criminality due to bonds of loyalty (sometimes familial as well as ethnic and racial) and threats of reprisal against anyone who informs, gang members fit both the convict-revolutionary and the serial-killer mold in some important respects. Defined by race and by region, these gangs emerged during the civil rights–era conflicts of the 1950s and 1960s but became a dominant force in California prisons in the 1970s as the old convict culture collapsed and hopes of political activism died.[19]

It is clear that for much of the period of mass incarceration, an overwhelming majority of California's prisoners have felt compelled to join the gangs to bring some measure of predictability, order, and safety to their lives. Authorities have long accommodated this gang order by placing new prisoners in their first cell assignments with other prisoners on the basis of race and by locking down California prisons on a racial basis.[20]

But if gang membership is ubiquitous, affiliation tells us little about the risk of future violence. Gang membership is thought to imply a willingness to participate in gang fights on yards

and in dining halls; in general, gangs are thought to ban social-
izing with members of other gangs and thus of other races.[21]
Yet within this vast system of racial gang organization, only a
small portion of prisoners are considered by prison officials to
pose threats. This leaves enormous discretion on the part of
prison staff with respect to which prisoners are housed in the
SHU units. Convict-revolutionaries and serial killers may be
few in number, but they are highly visible. The number of truly
active and dangerous gang members, in contrast, is difficult to
estimate and impossible to confirm. Ironically, this has had the
effect of minimizing the due process burden on California; because prison gangs are secretive and willing to kill informants,
little actual evidence of gang membership can be expected.
Therefore the case for placing the prisoner in supermax is
usually thin, but the impact on the individual is catastrophic,
according to Keramet Reiter:

> Inmates transferred to the SHU for prison gang affiliation
> are normally given an indeterminate term. This means that
> the inmate will remain in the SHU for the duration of his
> prison term unless the inmate "drops out" of the prison gang
> by successfully completing what is referred to as a "debrief-
> ing" process. As one inmate succinctly testified, "the only
> way [a prison gang member] can get out of [the SHU] is to
> debrief, parole, or just die of old age."[22]

Long before the deployment of supermax, the Supreme Court
recognized that prisoners facing disciplinary segregation had
the right to contest the evidence at a hearing and to be assisted
by another inmate or prison staff member if the case was "un-
duly complicated," given the prisoner's educational status. Prisoners are also entitled to a written decision regarding their case,
including a summary of the evidence the decision was based

on.[23] In *Helms v. Hewitt* (decided in 1983, at the outset of mass incarceration, then revisited in 1987), the court held that when prison authorities are segregating an inmate for general institutional security, not as discipline for an infraction, the Constitution gives the prisoner much less procedural protection.

> Due process, in the administrative context, merely requires that the prison officials provide the inmate with some notice of the charges against him and an opportunity to present [the inmate's] views to the prison official charged with deciding whether to transfer [the inmate] to administrative segregation.[24]

In the context of indeterminate administrative segregation in California's version of a supermax, the stakes are very high. Like "witches" in earlier times, contemporary prison gangs are endowed with presumptive power by both prison officials and prisoners, who attribute otherwise unexplained problems to them. And as with alleged witches, the accusation that a prisoner is an active gang member provides enormous opportunities for self-serving and harsh punishment of enemies within the prison population. If a non–gang member is falsely accused and segregated to the SHU, he has no information about the gang necessary to satisfy the requirement of "debriefing" for exit. Recognizing the mismatch between truth and consequences in the SHU, Judge Henderson finds that due process requires more:

> Accordingly, it is our conclusion that, in order to satisfy due process, an inmate may not be confined to the SHU for gang affiliation unless the record contains "some factual information" from which the IGI [Institutional Gang Investigator] and classification committee "can reasonably conclude that the information was reliable."[25]

In theory this allows courts to evaluate the ultimate judgment and its relationship to the evidence. In practice, however, only a handful of California SHU inmates have won transfer due to court action.

In the mid-1990s, as the fear of violent crime as a political force was peaking in California and as frightening figures such as serial sex offender and murderer Richard Allen Davis dominated media coverage,[26] a federal trial court was reluctant to go too far in challenging the necessity for supermax-style prisons. Nevertheless, facts brought to light in the *Madrid* trial about the situation of prisoners with serious mental illnesses when locked into the SHU pointed to the fundamental flaws underlying the security logic of supermax. Such prisoners inevitably worsen in the harsh isolation regime, as documented in *Madrid*:

Inmate 1, whose records indicate a history of psychiatric illness as an adolescent, was placed in the SHU in November 1990. By April 1992, he was suffering from a paranoid hallucinatory psychosis. He was convinced his food was being poisoned, and was drinking from his toilet and refusing to eat. He reported having auditory and visual hallucinations, claimed that a microphone had been placed in his cell, and was experiencing extreme anxiety. Pelican Bay staff initially asserted that he was malingering, but then also prescribed powerful antipsychotic medicine. A visiting psychiatrist concluded that he had classical symptoms of paranoid schizophrenia and was not being manipulative. On August 28, 1992, he was admitted to the infirmary on suicide watch. At that time, a staff psychiatrist diagnosed him as suffering from chronic undifferentiated schizophrenia and recommended that he be transferred to CMF-Vacaville for evaluation and treatment. When Dr. Grassian interviewed him on September 17, 1992, Inmate 1 was still in the SHU, actively psychotic and delusionally fearful of being killed. He was eventually transferred to CMF-Vacaville in November, where his clinical state dramatically improved and his psychotic symptoms remitted. The evaluation there indicated that he was: "an immature, needy emotionally underdeveloped young man who simply cannot cope psychologically with the situation that he has made for himself and which he probably never anticipated. . . . He is genuinely afraid, even panicked, by the Pelican Bay SHU, which seems to have crushed him." Because his mental state improved at CMF-Vacaville, he was transferred back to the SHU in March of 1993. When Dr. Grassian interviewed him a second time in May of 1993, Inmate 1 had again degenerated into a psychotic state; he was agitated, terrified, and hallucinatory.

The treatment of prisoners with mental illness inside the SHU—both the force used against them and the lack of medical care for their treatable conditions—became the core of the cruel-and-unusual-punishment finding against California. The case of one inmate in particular, whose torturelike treatment was described in great detail by Judge Henderson, brought together several of the most troubling features of the SHU regime at Pelican Bay. Vaughn Dortch was a severely mentally ill prisoner whose self-abuse, including smearing himself and his cell with his own feces, led to his being "extracted" from his cell by a special team of correctional officers who then proceeded to place him in a bath deliberately filled with water hot enough to scald, as described in the *Madrid* opinion:

Vaughn Dortch, a mentally ill inmate, suffered second- and third-degree burns over one-third of his body when he was given a bath in scalding water in the prison infirmary. The week before the incident Dortch bit an officer. Dortch had also created a nuisance by smearing himself and his cell with his own fecal matter. Although there was a shower near Dortch's cell, which would have provided a more efficient method of cleaning Dortch than a bath (even assuming Dortch was uncooperative), the officers instead forcibly escorted Dortch to a bathtub in the SHU infirmary, located some distance away in another complex.

The SHU was built on 1970s nightmares. Vaughn Dortch's story, which goes on for paragraphs more in the opinion, paints a picture of how profoundly those images deformed correctional practice, which then adopted medieval tortures that constituted cruel and unusual punishment.

Traditionally, even directors of maximum-security prisons imagined a "normal" routine wherein staff and inmates go about their business in common corridors, tier hallways, and program spaces. This assumes acceptance by all of a basic legitimacy to the prison's order, if only to avoid worse trouble. At times of emergency, such prisons could be locked down, temporarily becoming supermax, although it then strains every resource of the prison to maintain essential services such as food. Supermax prisons by contrast presume a permanent state of emergency. They assume the prisoner is an unrelenting enemy, just as in the new war prisons, Guantánamo, Abu Ghraib, and the rest.[27] All war-prison inmates are enemies who can be neither treated nor deterred. Unlike traditional prisoners of war or wounded combatants, the new war prisoners ("detainees") remain presumptively a threat even in custody, leaving no legitimate prison order to be maintained or respected.

The objectification of SHU prisoners as gang members has helped institutionalize the war model of California corrections. Unlike the prisoners sent to the SHU for a serious disciplinary violation, the gang member is a permanent enemy whose good behavior can never reassure, who must always be neutralized.

Because killing them is unacceptable under current legal norms, we must resort to permanent incapacitation, using a detention regime that removes any potential for the prisoner to continue to operate as an enemy. Unlike earlier strategies, which offered prisoners some form of life in which they could participate and seek to establish a more tolerable existence or even early release, the California-style supermax dispenses with all inducements or explanations. Its order is maintained simply by its technologies of control and abundant applications of force, sustained for as long as the law will permit.[28]

No aspect of the SHU regime disturbed the court more than the reliance on raw physical force, especially weapons. The control practices at Pelican Bay were strikingly warlike. Despite the signature high-tech surveillance equipment and the pod design, actual practice as documented in the *Madrid* litigation showed little reliance on surveillance to pacify prisoners. The method of choice was organized physical violence.

At the center of the SHU's control strategy was the "cell extraction." In this procedure, a phalanx of prison officers wearing layers of military-grade body armor and helmets, firing Tasers and sometimes "gas guns" (gas-powered shotguns that fire clusters of plastic pieces with enough force to cause temporarily disabling pain but generally not enough to injure or kill), burst into the cell and "secure" the prisoner. They then place him in a "fetal restraint position," actually a reverse fetal position with legs and arms bent painfully behind him and chained together. Extractions often ended with prisoners naked and injured, chained inside cages in the front sections of the prison, exposed to officers and other staff. The *Madrid* court found a pattern of intentional injury as a standard part of cell extractions—beatings with or without weapons.

The elements of mutilation and display recall the eighteenth-century "rituals of the scaffold," but they coexist with a bureaucratic form of organization, even if that bureaucracy is at times managed chaotically.[29] California's supermax system shared these features with the Southern plantation prisons at the center of the first wave of successful prison-condition court cases in the 1960s and 1970s. As discussed in chapter 1, California had been at the forefront of modern rationalization of corrections in the middle of the twentieth century, which formed the national standard to which the Southern prisons were held. But by the 1990s, when Pelican Bay opened, the "civil war" between prison officers and a handful of revolutionary prisoners had been extended to the more than two thousand prisoners at Pelican Bay and Corcoran SHU, and it would eventually be brought to the hundreds of thousands of Californians confined in state prisons during the 1990s and 2000s.

As California prisons underwent the transformation to mass incarceration, the bureaucratic structure created in the post–World War II period remained but was unanchored from any penal goals beyond incapacitation. The midlevel managers who emphasized security in the new prisons were responding to security nightmares of the early 1970s. But in the 1980s and 1990s, total incapacitation was being deployed against a population defined more by mental illness and gang identification than violent behavior. Among the most damning of Judge Henderson's findings in the *Madrid* case was that the cell extractions, the beatings, and the long periods of physical punishment by restraining prisoners in painful positions were not impulsive actions motivated by anger but were standard practices carried out under inhumane rules.

Cell extractions were ordered only in response to sustained refusal to obey orders and so were designed to overcome resistance, but the court found that the excessive level of force went beyond any reasonable security concerns. For example, cell extractions at Pelican Bay almost always included use of the electric shock gun, or Taser, whether the prisoner resisted or not. It wasn't that the department had failed to provide guidelines.

No, the rules *required* Taser use before entry by the extraction team. This remarkable mandate reveals a system not of "wild justice" or vengeance of the outraged sovereign or individual guards, but a system of risk management in which any risk posed by the prisoner is unacceptable, no matter how slight. The prison officer as citizen is juxtaposed with the prisoner as enemy. This is no longer a penal strategy; it's a war.

Judge Henderson found that cell extractions with weapons, combined with punishments like shackling in contorted positions, violate the core values of the Eighth Amendment. He was even more adamant in rejecting the forms of punitive detention that followed cell extractions:

Leaving inmates in outdoor cages for any significant period— as if animals in a zoo—offends even the most elementary notions of common decency and dignity. It also fails to serve any legitimate penological purpose in any kind of weather, much less cold and rainy weather. The fact that it occurred at all exhibits a callous and malicious intent to inflict gratuitous humiliation and punishment.[30]

The court was bound to accord prison managers and correctional officers due regard for their "unenviable task," but the warlike style of management in Pelican Bay belied any meaningful notion of "safe custody," even assuming that prisoners were uniformly dangerous. The most sweeping findings in *Madrid* were against the use of force. Finding the routine cell extractions unconstitutional, the court ordered revamped procedures for addressing inmate disobedience, as well as improved staff training in handling prisoners with serious mental illnesses. The court did not find, however, that the many abuses documented were inevitable results of supermax incarceration, instead concluding that they were the results of failures by prison management to train and adequately oversee correctional officers and their tactics. The court ordered the state to revise procedures and began an oversight that would last until 2011. This process was largely successful in removing the most abusive practices of the SHU. In public statements since 2005, Judge Henderson has observed that the reduction in the use of force at the Pelican Bay SHU is one of his proudest accomplishments, and in March 2011, the court officially terminated the jurisdiction it held over Pelican Bay, stating that "the Court is proud of the work done during the life of this case. Pelican Bay was once a place where prison officials used force 'for the very purpose of inflicting punishment and pain.' "[31]

* * *

The legal battle against supermax turned out to be a critical part of a broader struggle on behalf of people with mental illnesses imprisoned through mass incarceration policies, many of whom were placed in supermax custody because of the psychological disintegration that follows lack of treatment. Even after rehabilitation had been abandoned, one might have expected that the total surveillance and control would have allowed medical problems to be observed and addressed with great efficiency. But the opposite was true at Pelican Bay, which had opened without a credible system in place to deliver even minimal health care or mental health treatment. Judge Henderson quotes directly from one of the prisoners' expert witnesses in *Madrid*:

> We agree with Dr. Start's opinion that "[t]he fact that a new prison with contemporary medical facilities nevertheless could be so shockingly deficient in its provision of health care is . . . a terrible indictment of the defendants, and compellingly illustrates what . . . is their stunning indifference to the health care needs of the prisoners at Pelican Bay."[32]

This was not a failure of bureaucracy. Health and mental health care were lacking not due to a chaotic and underfunded system but because the California Department of Corrections did not view them as a priority during the construction of the gigantic, carefully planned SHUs.[33] The supermaxes were not underfunded. The planners of this high-cost public capital investment overwhelmingly focused on building a security utopia for prison officers. The bodies and minds of prisoners were thought of as threats to security in every possible way, but the threats those bodies and minds faced from the prisons were not thought about at all. It was as if prisoners' bodies were so dominated by their status as offenders (suggested by the popular use of terms like *predators* to describe people in prison, regardless of their actual crimes) that they didn't contain human organs subject to disease. While prison architects provided enough physical space for health care to be delivered to SHU prisoners, they never hired the professional staff or created the institutional routines that would be necessary to deliver it. Specifically, very little attention was paid to mental health screening and treatment for prisoners just entering the Pelican Bay SHU, even though prisoners with serious mental illnesses were especially likely to be sent to the SHU by officials at other prisons, who not surprisingly found them difficult management problems. Despite the clear necessity and the opportunity to identify those with vulnerability at the outset and track their mental health, the Pelican Bay SHU routines favored getting prisoners into their cells whether or not the intense isolation supermax regime there was likely to rapidly destroy the mental health of an already deeply ill prisoner or push an inmate's borderline mental health into serious mental illness.

As Judge Henderson observes in the *Madrid* decision, Pelican Bay opened and operated "for almost three years," without "an organized screening system at all."[34] To evaluate changes and to deliver necessary treatments, modern prisons also require the presence of psychiatric professionals qualified to undertake the necessary evaluations and treatments. Judge Henderson concludes:

> Until April 1992—almost 2 and ½ years after the prison opened—there was no resident psychiatrist at Pelican Bay with the exception of a psychiatrist who submitted his resignation after working for one month. Instead, defendants attempted to obtain visiting psychiatrists from other institutions for two to five days each month. . . . However, even this sparse coverage was not always obtained.[35]

Another key to mental health management in prisons is to obtain legal permission to medicate prisoners who are experiencing serious mental illness but, due to their own symptoms, refuse treatment. State laws and constitutional precedents require involuntary treatment to be carried out only under special procedures intended to determine if the patient is an imminent threat to himself or others due to his symptoms. Such procedures are crucial to any institution with a population likely to experience episodes of severe mental illness. As Judge Henderson describes the situation in the *Madrid* opinion:

> At Pelican Bay, there are no protocols or procedures in place for administering involuntary psychiatric medication. Instead, inmates needing involuntary medication must be transferred to [California Medical Facility, the only existing correctional mental hospital in California at that time] for inpatient treatment. However, as noted, this process usually takes three days, and sometimes longer, during which time the inmate is not involuntarily medicated. Thus, inmates in acute distress often suffer for an extended period of time

before they receive treatment that should be provided immediately. In short, defendants created a prison which, given its mission, size, and nature, would necessarily and inevitably result in an extensive demand for mental health services—perhaps more so than any other California facility; yet, at the same time, they scarcely bothered to furnish mental health services at all, and then only at a level more appropriate to a facility much smaller in size and modest in mission.[36]

Moreover, Henderson sees this failure to provide care as creating a particularly cruel twist for those who had wound up in the SHU primarily because of behavioral problems originating in their mental illnesses. They are "trapped in a Catch-22: they are too psychotic to consent to treatment, yet their psychosis makes them too 'dangerous' for a transfer to a facility where they could receive treatment that would potentially reduce their security risk."[37]

The plaintiffs in Madrid argued that the mental health effects of being in the supermax were themselves unconstitutional—cruel and unusual punishment. If the Eighth Amendment requires the prison to try to restore you to mental health, does it not also then prevent the prison from robbing you of your mental health in the first place? The plaintiffs had on their side powerful and largely unrebutted expert testimony that sustained confinement in supermax conditions of isolation, sensory deprivation, and total absence of activity can indeed cause an otherwise mentally stable individual to become mentally ill. But they faced the difficulty that California's complete commitment to incapacitation as the purpose of prison in general, and the supermax in particular, rendered risks to the prisoner a secondary concern. The court, necessarily deferential to the state's freedom of choice over prison policy, could not object to the balance of risks involved in placing persons presumed dangerous to prison officers in a situation that placed the prisoners at risk of becoming mentally ill:

> [The] general concept of segregating inmates for disciplinary or security reasons is a well established and penologically justified practice. . . . Defendants are thus entitled to design and operate the SHU consistent with the penal philosophy of their choosing, absent constitutional violations. . . . They may emphasize idleness, deterrence, and deprivation over rehabilitation. This is not a matter for judicial review or concern unless the evidence demonstrates that conditions are so extreme as to violate basic concepts of humanity and deprive inmates of a minimal level of life's basic necessities.[38]

In considering the constitutional status of supermax incarceration, Judge Henderson was not writing on a blank slate. In an earlier challenge to California's new general prison regime, *Touissaint v. McCarthy*,[39] the courts had rejected the claim that incarceration without any productive activity aimed at rehabilitation of the prisoner was inherently cruel and unusual. Thus purely incapacitative punishment had been upheld as a constitutional choice in decisions clearly binding on Judge Henderson in the *Madrid* case. What the SHU provided was a new opportunity for courts to consider California's commitment to total incapacitation. Because total incapacitation is intrinsically likely to cause mental harm to some prisoners, the court faced a difficult task in stating constitutional limits. Any prison confinement may have a deleterious impact on the mental state of prisoners, for reasons that are self-evident. Especially for those facing long sentences, as the court noted, "depression, hopelessness, frustration, and other such psychological states may well prove to be inevitable byproducts."[40] In the end, the court concluded that only those already suffering

from mental illness were at such extreme risk of complete breakdown that confining them in a supermax was intrinsically cruel
and unusual punishment.

* * *

Substantively, the *Madrid* complaint differed from much modern prison-condition litigation. Its stated goal was not reform
of a state prison system that was failing to produce a normally
competent version of an accepted strategy of punishment. Instead, the plaintiffs were seeking to call out as unconstitutional
what they viewed as a new prison regime. In an interview a
few years after *Madrid*, psychologist Terry Kupers, who had
worked closely with the prisoners' legal team as an expert, describes the mixed success of this strategy:

> ... *Madrid* was a "split decision." After all, the plaintiffs ar-
> gued that supermax confinement is entirely unconstitutional,
> the court ruled that they failed to prove (to the satisfaction
> of the court) that supermax confinement is unconstitutional
> per se, but did find that for prisoners suffering from serious
> mental illness long-term segregation is cruel and unusual.
> Federal courts in other states have determined that the
> *Madrid* decision must be applied in their jurisdictions.[41]

Judge Henderson did find certain aspects of the California
supermax regime to violate the Eighth Amendment's bar on
"cruel and unusual" punishment, and he also began to question the arbitrary administrative power of selection for the
supermax. But although it did provide relief to one class of
prisoners—those with preexisting mental health conditions—
Madrid must be seen overall as a missed opportunity to disable
an anchor of the regime of mass incarceration and its underlying tendencies toward inhuman, degrading, and ultimately
torturous conditions.

Thus the solution of the mid-1990s was to leave states free to continue the supermax strategy but to create legal and regulatory limits to the way they exercised power over prisoners. This compromise has remained intact. Supermax has become an integral part of mass incarceration. The two will survive or fall together. Indeed, within months of the *Brown v. Plata* decision, SHU prisoners launched a series of disciplined hunger strikes that won an unusual measure of public attention and support. The state has thus far continued to shrink from any serious effort to revise its heavy reliance on SHUs, just as it has continued to resist full implementation of the *Plata* prison-population-reduction order.[42]

Perhaps the most promising aspects of the *Madrid* decision were those that highlighted the danger that the California supermax system posed to the *dignity* of prisoners. Most of the Eighth Amendment–based rights to certain levels of prison conditions announced by courts during the high tide of prison reform in the 1970s and 1980s were articulated in terms of specific changes in prison conditions, but underlying them all is constitutional protection for human dignity, as is made clear in Judge Henderson's decision:

> By virtue of their conviction, inmates forfeit many of their constitutional liberties and rights: they are isolated in prisons, and subject to stringent restrictions that govern every aspect of their daily lives. Nonetheless, those who have transgressed the law are still fellow human beings—most of whom will one day return to society. Even those prisoners at the "bottom of the social heap . . . have, nonetheless, a human dignity." . . . In recognition of this fundamental principle, our jurisprudence is clear: while incarceration may extinguish or curtail many rights, the Eighth Amendment's protection against cruel and unusual punishment still retains its "full force" behind prison doors.

Confronting a particularly aberrant and grotesque version of supermax incarceration in Pelican Bay in the early 1990s, Judge Henderson can be excused for not recognizing that reforming abuses could not make mass incarceration or its supermax prisons compatible with human dignity. But using the classic judicial method of stating a hypothetical case, Judge Henderson articulates a dignity-based limit on punishment that eerily anticipates the conditions that would come with chronic hyper-overcrowding to be addressed in the decisions following *Madrid*: "Sedating all inmates with a powerful medication that leaves them in a continual stupor would arguably reduce security risks; however, such a condition of confinement would clearly fail constitutional muster."[43]

In supermax incarceration, punishment is no longer the legally intended loss of liberty, access to family and friends, and the opportunity to develop oneself. It has transformed into something more profound—the denial of a recognizable human existence and the reduction to a pure biological existence, one that political theorists might call "bare life."[44]

The decision in *Madrid v. Gomez* began to illuminate this danger, which most scholarly critics of mass incarceration had missed. Imprisoning people to achieve general incapacitation, with no concern for individual criminal history or risk, denies their humanity. A prison system organized on that basis cannot preserve the human dignity of its prisoners—or its employees. In the long run, it becomes a humanitarian disaster. To see that disaster in its full scale, we must move beyond the special problem of the supermax to the broader inhumanity of mass incarceration.

3

Engines of Madness

Coleman v. Wilson

By the late 1980s, the concentration of people with untreated mental illness inside state prisons was becoming noticeable, and it was the subject of a new round of lawsuits launched by a non-profit prisoner-rights organization, the Prison Law Office, on behalf of California prisoners. The *Madrid v. Gomez* case, filed in 1991 and decided in 1995, focused on solitary confinement in supermax SHUs and raised one set of connections between mass incarceration and this group of prisoners, including the seriously psychotic ones especially targeted for supermax in California. *Madrid* highlighted the danger that supermax prison conditions pose for prisoners with existing mental illness and showed how common those so afflicted were becoming in a system that had made no provision for them.

However, the Pelican Bay prisoners in question were just a fraction of a far larger population of prisoners with serious mental illness housed at all security levels in California's vast archipelago of lockups. They might not face the aggravating conditions of near total isolation (with or without a cellmate), but they still had special needs that had to be met in order to prevent their illnesses from deepening. Yet even lower-security prisons, intended to provide at least some rehabilitative services, lacked the basic elements of mental health care.

This mismatch—concentrating the mentally ill in prisons based on a nonpsychological view of prisoners—was at the center of a second case brought at almost the same time as the *Madrid* case. *Coleman v. Wilson* was a class action on behalf of *all* prisoners with a serious mental illness alleging that California's failure to provide adequate mental health care in its prisons violated the Eighth and Fourteenth Amendments. In 1995, shortly after the *Madrid* decision, Judge Lawrence Karlton ruled in favor of the prisoners and ordered a sweeping reform of prison mental health services in California. Looking beyond the nightmare of the SHU, *Coleman* showed that untreated mental illness was a routine and widespread feature of mass incarceration. The ruling, undoubtedly the largest and most complex court order concerning mental health care in history, gave the prisoners and their advocates a complete legal victory, but the order has not yet been effectively implemented despite a quarter-century struggle.

Judge Karlton ordered California to shoulder its responsibilities by establishing a comprehensive system of mental health care capable of accomplishing all six elements of the constitutionally minimal standard of care described in his opinion.

(1) a systematic program for screening and evaluating inmates to identify those in need of mental health care; (2) a treatment program that involves more than segregation and close supervision of mentally ill inmates; (3) employment of a sufficient number of trained mental health professionals; (4) maintenance of accurate, complete and confidential mental health treatment records; (5) administration of psychotropic medication only with appropriate supervision and

periodic evaluation; and (6) a basic program to identify, treat, and supervise inmates at risk for suicide.[1]

Karlton's decision implicitly demands an individualized understanding of inmates with mental illnesses. Prisons would have to be responsive to individuals' diagnoses and treatment plans rather than treating them as an undifferentiated mass to be held in captivity.

Using the wedge of mental illness, *Coleman*, even more than *Madrid*, began to define mass incarceration as the source of unconstitutional conditions. The concentration of people with mental illness was not an aberration. The mentally ill, according to the *Coleman* suit, were a substantial and routine part of the correctional system's target custodial population. Once the presence of people with serious and untreated mental illness is acknowledged, concentrating those people in spaces lacking the rudiments of care becomes a major human rights scandal.

* * *

By the mid-1990s, critics were thinking about mass incarceration as a question of quantitative excess: too many prisoners, too many prisons, too many people on parole and probation. In this view, mass incarceration was simply modern corrections unhinged and unchecked. But a qualitative change had happened as well. A major goal of modern corrections—attending to the psychology and psychopathology of prisoners, central to the whole enterprise since at least World War I—had been abandoned.

Mental health care in prison had required a base of knowledge about each prisoner—paying attention to "the soul of prisoners." Based on eugenics and social work, this individualizing attitude has played an important role in American corrections, providing the understanding needed for nonviolent control and acting as a constraint on the severity of punishment in prison. California became a global leader in all aspects of the movement, both the enlightened (therapeutic communities) and the despicable (involuntary eugenic sterilization). That changed abruptly in the middle of the 1970s. In a few years, the state went from being the most committed to this medical model to being the most extreme in its rejection of it. The consequences would be proportionately severe. Other states, especially in the South, would come to rival California in their zeal to build more prisons and incarcerate more prisoners in the 1980s and 1990s, but no other did so as heedlessly with regard to how prison order would be established and decency sustained. When mass incarceration came to the former Confederacy, it could rely on local cultures of prison control such as chain gangs that had little or no footing in medical models or rehabilitation, and in many respects reached back to slavery for their institutional inspirations.[2] Human dignity was not a value of importance in those cultures, to say the least, but ironically their ability to maintain a public order and, through prison labor, a more active prison life probably put a floor on basic decency that California fell through. Having abandoned their modern correctional tools for controlling prisoners as individuals and myopically focused on incapacitating criminals presumed to be permanently dangerous, California prisons were rapidly becoming institutions for collecting and intensifying mental health problems, veritable engines of madness.

Coleman revealed that California's turn to mass incarceration meant abandoning the long history shared between prisons and the mental hospitals. Prisons and asylums emerged in their modern form in the early nineteenth century amid widespread criticism of jails and workhouses for carelessly mingling the criminal, the poor, and the mentally ill. Optimism ran high about the capacity of new strategies to transform the deviant citizen.[3] In the late nineteenth and early twentieth centuries, the project of prisons drew even closer to that of asylums, as psychiatrists and psychologists became influential inside prisons and prison reformers characterized most criminal offenders as psychological deviants in need of rehabilitative treatment. The institutions of probation, parole, and juvenile courts and detention centers arose in response.[4]

In the post–World War II era, the American states that were most progressive on penal policy (New York, California, Michigan, and Illinois) invested in new prisons and new techniques to create capacity within prisons for dealing with the psychological deviance thought to be driving criminal behavior. In the 1970s, as outlined in previous chapters, the relationship between prisons and asylums changed again as state prison systems shifted away from the objective of rehabilitation. In California, the key elements of the postwar legal framework of rehabilitation—indeterminate sentencing and an adult parole authority with power to release rehabilitated prisoners—were abolished by the Determinate Sentence Law of 1976. Now the legally defined purpose of prison was punishment. Release was no longer tied to individualized assessment; the entire sentence had to be served whether the inmate reformed or not.[5] It didn't matter whether states adopted fixed sentencing or nominally stayed with indeterminate sentences and parole release; psychological factors, once the bread and butter of correctional thinking, became irrelevant to the length or conditions of imprisonment.[6] Prison planners now not only gave inmates no incentive for reform but created conditions that discouraged it.

By the late 1980s, California's prisons and courts had been purged of more than two centuries of psychological insight. Mental illness was still seen as a cause of criminal behavior (indeed the psychotic serial killer became a staple of the common sense about prisons and crime), but it was no longer a significant legal obstacle to harsh punishment by diminishing responsibility or suggesting amenability to reform via treatment. The barriers that law and discretion had placed against imprisoning people with serious mental illnesses when treatment alternatives were available had largely disappeared.[7] Instead of sending these people to hospitals that in their lack of treatment were little better than jails, California's mass incarceration policies were drawing increasing numbers of people with serious mental illness to prisons that offered no mental health treatment or rehabilitative programs.

The transformations on the medical side—the asylums—were in some respects even more dramatic. In the years after World War II, prison officials in progressive states including California made mental hospitals their ideal for what prisons could be; by the 1970s however, state mental hospitals were well on their way to being viewed as prisons without legal justification for holding their inmates.[8] Poor conditions and lack of proper care in many mental hospitals, as well as more profound cultural doubts about the usefulness of treatment and about the dangerousness of people with mental illness (not to mention budget cuts and indifference), led to massive releases of patients, some of whom had been confined in hospitals for decades. State mental hospital systems shrank to a fraction of their former size. As states built the infrastructure for mass incarceration over the next two decades, it was perhaps inevitable that many with untreated mental health problems would be swept into the courts and prisons.

This was clearly not an intended transfer of populations. The hospital population of the 1970s was disproportionately white, female, and older than the prison population then or since. For reformers, the closure of the asylums was supposed to be followed by the development of a community-based mental health system that would support patients and their families without requiring isolation and custody. When state governments turned out to be far more interested in cutting social spending and private developers were uninterested in creating housing or treatment space for people living with serious mental illnesses, it was perhaps inevitable that many of those without family support or money of their own would be criminalized. There appears to have been no rapid turn to imprisonment. People with mental illness needed to accumulate lots of minor convictions over a number of years before ending up in state prisons. States were expanding their prisons and using minor offenses to fill them. Intentionally set up without mental health services and located far from cities, where mental health professionals tend to live, the new prisons became asylums without doctors.[9] But while actual asylums had become a scandal by the 1950s, mass-incarceration prisons were a black hole into which the mentally ill disappeared without protest from professionals, journalists, or politicians.

Given this context, *Coleman v. Wilson* was an astounding success despite the state's failure to comply. By granting legal recognition to prisoners with serious mental illness as a class with a shared right to adequate mental health care, *Coleman* opened a window into the mass incarceration prison. California's systematic lack of mental health screening and treatment had made the problem invisible. But since 1990, the court's jurisdiction over members of the *Coleman* class has made these prisoners visible, placed the prison system under a mandate to track and treat them, and by means of a special master in charge of implementing the court's orders, created an independent authority accountable for the fate of these prisoners.

Legal recognition of the class and appointment of a special master assured that the suffering of mentally ill prisoners was noticed and charted, even if not alleviated, but these improvements also exposed mass incarceration's fundamental contradictions. When mental illness that has led to sustained criminal conduct or violence in the past is left untreated, future crime and violence is likely. This seemingly obvious observation is one of the best-established propositions in the business of criminal-risk prediction.[10]

Judge Karlton's opinion highlights the fact that California's prisons had become the new asylums:

> In California . . . prisons have also become the repository of an enormous number of the state's mentally ill. Thus in the matter at bar one of defendants' experts estimated that on any given day there are probably between 13,000 and 18,000 inmates in California's prisons in need of treatment because they suffer from serious mental disorders.[11]

Mass incarceration had covered up the scale of the problem; its planners and administrators were simply not interested, so most of the mentally ill remained undetected. The *Coleman* class action led to the identification of a large and growing number of such prisoners. Professional staff and procedures to screen and track prisoners mandated by the court now made it possible to identify those with serious mental illness, who therefore qualified for class membership. Describing the work that remained in 1995 to identify all class members, Judge Karlton notes:

> The consultants found that "[a] large number of unidentified individuals in the general population, were they to be screened, would be diagnosable with the same serious disorders and exhibit related symptoms. Given the size of the unidentified population (over 57,000 at the time of the survey), even the small base-rate of 7% for the four serious disorders amounts to over 4,000 undetected SMD [serious mental disorder] individuals."[12]

Despite the legal victory for prisoners, *Coleman v. Wilson*'s promise of mental health care for people with serious mental disorders in prison has remained unfulfilled for eighteen years as of this writing. Despite millions of dollars of investment in mental health capacity, massive overcrowding means that conditions for prisoners with mental illness were little better in 2010 (or now) than they were in 1995 when *Coleman* was decided. It is the unremedied suffering of prisoners (along with the parallel crisis in physical health, to which we turn in the next chapter) that has come to condemn mass incarceration itself, and not just particular prison conditions that it produces, as unconstitutional. The lawyers for the *Coleman* class, aided since 1995 by a special master operating as an arm of the court itself and charged with collecting data on mentally ill prisoners, have returned to court repeatedly seeking to have the remedy finally put in place. Their efforts culminated in the 2009 population cap ordered by the special three-judge court in *Coleman-Plata v. Schwarzenegger*. The powerful documentation of the state's continued failure to care for those with serious mental illness would be some of the most damning evidence in favor of the prisoners when the Supreme Court decided the state's appeal of the population cap in *Brown v. Plata*.

The *Coleman* litigation's focus on people in prison with serious mental illness could have reinforced the historically powerful popular association of mental illness with criminality. The misperception that people with mental illness commonly become violent has long been a popular argument for confining them. Evidence that many prisoners were now diagnosed with serious mental illnesses could have ratified the decision to keep them confined. However, the litigation's focus on the unmet treatment needs of prisoners revealed the patients to be mostly persons at risk, not threats to others. No fact about California's prisons better illustrated this than the inability of prisoners who wanted treatment for their active mental disorders to receive it, even when the disorders presented clear problems for staff and other prisoners as well as the affected inmates.

Judge Karlton observes as much, quoting from then-current evidence before the court that is consistent with quite recent reports:[13]

> In February 1992, the waiting list to see a psychiatrist after initial screening was over 400 inmates at the reception center at Wasco State Prison; delays lasted up to three months and had "escalated to the point where inmates were cutting their wrists just to receive medication."[14]

While many of the failings in 1995 were thought to be solvable by improved staffing, the system's ability to hire sufficient mental health staff would continue to lag behind the growth of the prison population and their needs, a problem exacerbated by overcrowding. This failure would soon come to have its own index: prisoner suicides, many of them committed by untreated sufferers of torturous mental illnesses. California's once psychiatrically sophisticated prisons had become places of grave psychiatric suffering with a suicide rate among prisoners in 2006 that was 80 percent above average. In absolute numbers approximately a prisoner per week committed suicide, and more than 70 percent of those suicides were estimated to be preventable if adequate treatment were available.[15]

The legal visibility of untreated prisoners with serious mental illnesses has moved the courts but, so far, not the public. When it comes to criminal justice, public opinion has a long lag time; it changes very slowly. Because of the high level of violent crime from the early 1960s through the early 1990s, people continue to think of the United States as a high-crime society,[16] despite two decades of sustained reductions that have brought violent crime to pre-1960s levels in many large cities that had once been epicenters of violence. Popular perceptions of crime are only now beginning to reflect this new awareness. Convict-revolutionaries and drifting serial killers provided archetypes or folk devils around which an extremely pessimistic mind-set about prisons and prisoners coalesced. Lacking any public confidence in experts to determine who the next George Jackson or Charles Manson might be, the public has maintained a commitment to general and categorical exclusion of repeat offenders through long prison sentences.

Supermax prisons were conceived as impermeable structures within which to contain an unchanging risk. Mass incarceration's withdrawal of rehabilitation efforts made evidence about the progress of individual prisoners irrelevant and unavailable. Whether or not they had victimized anyone by their crime, prisoners with serious mental illnesses were themselves victims of a system that had abdicated its responsibility to recognize the individual needs of prisoners. Judge Karlton makes the point incontrovertibly:

> It is apparent that due to a systemic failure to provide adequate mental health care, thousands of class members suffer present injury and are threatened with great injury in the future. The court concludes that the record in this case demonstrates beyond reasonable debate the objective component of plaintiffs' Eighth Amendment claim.[17]

The *Coleman* litigation generated a flow of images of prisoners suffering the torments of serious mental illness in a setting *designed* to drive even sane people crazy. Much of the case against California Department of Corrections came from the department's own files. A bona fide bureaucracy (unlike the states that had been found deficient in their record keeping during the 1970s and 1980s), the department had a formal chain of command and subordinates who dutifully reported to the leadership on the very real problems they faced in the mental health arena.

A memorandum written by Department of Corrections

lawyers for the top leadership that was quoted by Judge Karlton in the *Coleman* decision provided "smoking gun" evidence
for the sometime elusive subjective element of Eighth Amendment violations (the requirement of "deliberate indifference"):

> [t]he need to assess [inmates backlogged awaiting transfer
> for mental health services] is urgent. Seriously mentally ill
> inmates who do not receive needed treatment can worsen
> severely, losing most or all of their ability to function. Such
> inmates can also become suicidal or can pose significant
> risks to others or to the safety of the institution. In addition,
> the litigation facing the Department in this area, especially
> the Department-wide Coleman case, puts the Department at
> extreme liability risk if these inmates go untreated.[18]

Judge Karlton felt so strongly that the evidence in *Coleman* had
demonstrated actual knowledge of wrongdoing that he intentionally repeats his finding that:

> [T]he evidence of defendants' knowledge of the gross in-
> adequacies in their system is overwhelming. The risk of harm
> from these deficiencies is obvious. The actual suffering ex-
> perienced by mentally ill inmates is apparent. In the face of
> this reality, the court finds that defendants' conduct consti-
> tutes deliberate indifference to the serious medical needs of
> the plaintiff class.[19]

In demanding a prison system that can identify those at risk
for mental health degeneration and provide them therapeutic
measures necessary to prevent decompensation and suicide,
Coleman seemed to do no more than state the obvious requirements of the long-established constitutional right to adequate
health care in prison. A constitutionally adequate therapeutic
system obviously requires evaluating and monitoring each

prisoner individually, and in insisting that the Constitution requires this individualized knowledge, *Coleman* shook mass incarceration to its core. While proponents of mass incarceration may claim that containment alone reduces risk and that secure containment is all that the prison need aspire to, the result is unconstitutional. A constitutionally adequate prison must have a therapeutic system that correlates risk with the level of containment. In mass incarceration, knowledge of security is the only expertise available, but a constitutional prison requires psychological expertise. In creating *mass* incarceration, California abandoned the soul of the prisoner and lost its own.[20]

Between them, the *Madrid* and *Coleman* decisions, decided by parallel federal trial courts in 1995, were a turning point in the history of mass incarceration. As incarceration levels were hitting their peak, the two judges demanded that prisons respect basic human rights.

In *Madrid*, plaintiffs exposed the reliance of a supposedly humane high-tech regime for high-risk prisoners on abusive practices such as cell extractions; beatings; and torture with weapons, restraints, and cages. Judge Thelton Henderson's decision ordered the state to exempt the seriously mentally ill from *extra* brutality but left unchallenged the routine dehumanization of mass imprisonment in supermaxes. In *Coleman*, Judge Lawrence Karlton built on *Madrid* and began to put mass incarceration itself on trial.

4

Torture on the Installment Plan

Prisons Without Medicine in Plata v. Davis

The right to adequate health care in prison was well established by the 1980s, when mass incarceration took hold. In the landmark case of *Estelle v. Gamble,* decided in 1976, the Supreme Court held unequivocally that denying necessary medical care constitutes cruel and unusual punishment:

> An inmate must rely on prison authorities to treat his medical needs; if the authorities fail to do so, those needs will not be met. In the worst cases, such a failure may actually produce physical "torture or a lingering death," . . . the evils of most immediate concern to the drafters of the Amendment. In less serious cases, denial of medical care may result in pain and suffering which no one suggests would serve any penological purpose.[1]

This right to minimally adequate health care was easily met by most state prison systems in the 1970s because prison populations then (and earlier) were much younger than the general population and thus were healthier (though not when compared with people of their own age). Young populations are the least expensive to provide with health care. The older the prisoners are and the longer they're imprisoned, the more likely it is that their health will become a problem requiring treatment. The fact that in earlier periods the vast majority of prisoners were in prison for only a short time also made health care less of an issue. Mass incarceration changed both dimensions. Longer sentences pushed up the age range of the prison population. A third of California's prisoners are projected to be over fifty-five by 2030.[2] More incarceration of drug offenders may have increased the portion of the prison population with chronic illnesses. And with prisoners of all ages serving longer terms, the negative consequences of imprisonment on health have a greater opportunity to accumulate.

*　*　*

The system of mass incarceration that has developed in California over the past forty years is unique in the history of the modern prison in its degree of disassociation from the entire problem of disease and medical care. As with mental illness, the very things that define mass incarceration as a distinctive mode of punishment—its scale, its categorical nature, and its prioritization of custody over reform or rehabilitation—all predict that intensified health crises will be an inherent problem.

The size of the prison population matters because, as the absolute number of prisoners needing substantial medical treatment grows, the infrastructure necessary to deliver that level of care requires very costly investments and a substantial reworking of prison procedures. The rigidity of California's sentencing from the mid-1970s until *Brown v. Plata* (a feature of mass incarceration generally but, as always, more extreme in California) has meant that individuals with serious diseases requiring active management (which may diminish their criminal risk as well) are sentenced to prison rather than to alternatives including probation or home arrest where appropriate. Likewise, a prisoner in whom a serious chronic disease—AIDS, hepatitis, or cancer—emerges after imprisonment must remain in prison even as his health needs escalate and his criminal risk diminishes.[3]

The overwhelming priority of custody over transformation means that mass incarceration prisons lack the facilities and procedures to give efficient care to prisoners as individuals. More than the supermax horrors at Pelican Bay or the system-wide absence of mental health care, the failure to care about the physical health needs of a huge and long-serving population betrays the inhumanity of mass incarceration. The lack of health care in prisons implies a profound level of negligence and contempt, as if the bodies being incapacitated were not subject to the suffering accompanying injury, illness, and death—as if they were not human. The courts had long acknowledged that the absence of medical care could approximate torture and violate the Eighth Amendment. California's growing mismatch between its increasingly medically needy prisoners and its increasingly medically incompetent prisons would force the state to confront whether the accumulation of small injuries spread across thousands of prisoners constituted what we might call (adapting Louis Celine's famous characterization of death and injury in industrial work) "torture on the installment plan."

*   *   *

Nearly twenty years into mass incarceration in California, this health care crisis came to the fore in a class-action lawsuit filed in San Francisco federal court in 2001 by the Prison Law Office on behalf of all California prisoners with serious medical needs or the likelihood of developing them (that is, virtually all California prisoners). The case was assigned to Judge Thelton Henderson, the judge who had presided over the Pelican

Bay supermax case *Madrid v. Gomez* ten years earlier. *Plata v. Davis* (named after the first of its named plaintiffs and Governor Gray Davis) challenged the medical operations of the California prison system, claiming that California "does not and, with current systems and resources, cannot properly care for and treat prisoners in its custody," who therefore face an unacceptable and unconstitutional risk of "widespread harm, including severe and unnecessary pain, injury and death."[4]

The named plaintiffs in the *Plata* complaint were "ten California state prisoners . . . seriously injured because of defendants' deliberate indifference to their serious medical needs."[5] Some suffered from extremely serious diseases including heart failure and cancer, while many experienced initially relatively modest diseases or injuries or came to prison with problems easily cared for on the outside but which, through neglect and mismanagement inside, resulted in great pain and permanent disability. The plaintiffs were an ordinary set of human beings with ordinary human bodies. Their stories revealed a system that no longer recognized them as such.

A prime example is Marciano Plata, the lead plaintiff. Plata injured his back and knee in a fall while working in the kitchen at Calipatria State Prison in Imperial County, a mostly maximum-security (level IV) prison opened in 1992 to hold approximately 2,300 prisoners. Despite frequent requests to correctional officers and frontline prison health care personnel for assistance, it took almost two months for Plata to be seen by an orthopedic specialist who recommended arthroscopic surgery of the knee to repair a tear in the cartilage and stabilize the knee. His condition led to sharp pain and regular buckling of the knee. It took a year and a half for Plata to receive surgery, which almost certainly only occurred at all because Plata maintained an irrepressible campaign of requests and complaints through the proper bureaucratic channels, all documented in the record. But in an action that illustrated the power of frontline prison officers to overturn medical decisions, in direct disregard of instructions they had received from medical professionals at the nonprison hospital where the procedure had taken place, correctional officers forced him to walk on his just-operated-upon knee, causing great pain and further damage. No follow-up care was permitted. This was an act of cruel and unusual punishment, or simply torture.

Joseph Long, a twenty-four-year-old paraplegic, suffered severe pain and incontinence after the prison failed to assess or treat a bladder stone for more than ten months. As documented in the *Plata* complaint,

> In June 2000, while Mr. Long was incarcerated at Wasco State Prison Reception Center, defendant Dr. Bhaviesh Shah assessed Mr. Long and referred him to a urologist due to his history of bladder stones. Neither Dr. Shah, nor any other medical personnel at Wasco State Prison took any further steps to ensure that Mr. Long was actually seen by a urologist for the four months he was incarcerated at that facility. During this time, Mr. Long suffered from pain from his bladder stone and urinary tract infections. Despite his complaints about these problems and about the ineffectiveness of the antibiotics given to him, he never was examined by a specialist. . . .
>
> Mr. Long was transferred from Wasco to Salinas Valley State Prison on October 27, 2000, where he continued to have urinary tract and bladder infections and to complain about the debilitating pain of the infections and his need for further medical attention. Defendant Dr. Andrew Wong prescribed antibiotics to treat Mr. Long's infections but did not refer him to a urologist. Dr. Wong pursued this course of treatment despite the fact that Mr. Long exhibited persistent signs of infection and that Mr. Long complained of acute pain and had a history and symptoms of bladder stones. . . .

Mr. Long did not receive an examination by a urologist until April 11, 2001. On that date he underwent surgery at the Corcoran State Prison Acute Care Hospital. The surgeon, Dr. Dwivedi, removed a large bladder stone and expressed his opinion to Mr. Long that if Mr. Long was not paralyzed from the waist down he would have been unable to withstand the pain caused by such a large stone.[6]

Gilbert Aviles, another prisoner with paralysis, required daily catheterization to urinate. Aviles experienced repeated severe kidney infections aggravated after prison staff failed to regularly change his catheter; when they did bother to change it, they regularly did so with catheter parts that had expired and failed. After repeated cycles of disease by the time of the lawsuit, he suffered from chronic antibiotic-resistant infection.[7]

Paul Decasas, a prisoner with serious seizure disorder, suffered repeated seizures due to the failure of prison officials to provide his prescribed medication.

Doctors knew of his condition and permitted transfer. SATF [Substance Abuse Treatment Facility and State Prison, part of the massive prison complex in Corcoran, California] has no inpatient facility. No summary of his condition followed Decasas to [a different prison] including information regarding his medication needs. At [the new prison] he began to experience frequent seizures including documented ones on January 18, January 25, February 1, February 6, February 13, February 15, February 18, February 19, February 24, March 22, March 29, April 2, April 17, April 19, May 7, May 9, May 10, and May 15. Physicians at SATF failed to monitor or treat his condition and he was frequently not given his medication. He could not participate in the substance abuse treatment program he was transferred to SATF for.[8]

Steven Bautista experienced priapism, "a painful, persistent, and abnormal penile erection, unaccompanied by sexual desire or excitation," caused by an antidepressant prescribed for his diagnosed major depression. Physicians at High Desert State Prison allowed the priapism to continue for more than ninety-six hours before starting emergency treatment. The situation was resolved by surgery that left Bautista impotent, mutilated, and with urinary incontinence.[9]

Three themes—chronic illness, lack of individualized medical attention, and basic inhumanity—run through the stories of the *Plata* plaintiffs. These patterns, subtle at first, have the potential to reframe how we see prisons, prisoners, and crime prevention.

* * *

Shockingly and tellingly, the state of California never disputed the main claims made on behalf of the prisoners.[10] In June 2001, the parties entered a sweeping "stipulation for injunctive relief."[11] California agreed to undertake an extraordinary program of rebuilding and reorganizing state prisons designed to bring the state into constitutional compliance within three years. The state also agreed to a significant role for external monitoring, including a body of experts appointed by the court to advise the court on the "adequacy and implementation of the State's policies and to a score based audit system to be carried out by these external experts to determine when constitutional conditions had been established."

In 2005, more than three years into the stipulated agreement, Judge Henderson concluded that the required reforms would not be carried out unless the state was completely removed from control over prison health care. Again, shockingly, the state did not seriously contest the court's conclusion that it could not implement health care reforms internally. Judge Henderson appointed a receiver—a practice originating in bankruptcy and a far rarer and more drastic step than the more typical special master appointed to oversee institutional reforms ordered by a court. By that time, through his long experience with *Madrid* as well as *Plata*, Judge Henderson had become convinced that, even under the threat of federal contempt, California officials were not capable of reordering the prison health care system. The state correctional staff (not just frontline workers but bureaucrats further up the hierarchy) lacked not just the will to reform but even the capacity to imagine prisoners as human beings.

A stark example of this attitude was cited by Judge Henderson in his receivership opinion and order. During the first period when the parties were working together with the court to try to implement the stipulated agreement, a major challenge involved hiring health professionals for prisons sited far away from cities. The court held a hearing to explore waiving civil service and collective bargaining rules that were impeding the hiring. During the hearing, the defendant prison administrators claimed that they could not waive the procedures required by law without a sufficient emergency, something like the threat of losing federal funding unless hiring was done immediately.

> The Court responded that in one to six months "we would have 3 to 18 people dying. . . . I can't think of a bigger emergency." Even in light of the Court's concern, the witness continued to balk at the idea of doing any emergency contracting whatsoever for prisoner medical services.[12]

The stipulated agreement signed by the parties in 2001 was a plan to bring prison health care up to constitutional levels in three years. That reform has never happened and at this writing is still pending. Instead, a bit more than three years later, Judge Henderson's receivership opinion and order marked the beginning of the end of mass incarceration in California. Stripped of its administrative control over health care, one of the most expensive components of the vast prison system, and forced to accept the directives of an independent decision maker who had no political masters, California had partially lost control over its prisons—although not over its ability to send convicts to them.

In his receivership opinion and order, Judge Henderson for the first time in the litigation laid blame on California mass-incarceration policies as a whole: "In all fairness, the Court recognizes that the current administration inherited many of the problems identified above from past administrations, which must bear much of the blame for building California's vast prison system without regard for inmate medical care."[13]

The structural misalignment between prisoner health and prison design in California goes well beyond the confines of the Department of Corrections and has changed over time. In California, prison population growth has gone through three distinct phases.[14] In the first phase, prosecutors exercising their discretion sought prison time for a category of felons who might have received probation in the past. In the second phase, during the 1980s and early 1990s, the legislature increased prison sentences, especially for drug crimes. In the third phase, since the mid-1990s, additional prison population growth has come from mandatory sentencing rules, including the three-strikes law; very long sentences for violent crimes; and life sentences for murder.

The first two phases did not present much of a problem for health care costs. Even as prison populations began to swell in the 1980s, the vast majority of prisoners were young and serving relatively short sentences. The Reagan-Bush-era reescalation of the drug war probably increased the youth slant of the prison population in the 1980s in two ways, in adding more young prisoners and adding more prisoners serving relatively short sentences. The third phase, involving long mandatory sentences and parole denials, however, was a critical juncture at which the scale of health care needs began to rise exponentially. Just as healthy young adults are the tonic for any health insurance model, aging sick adults are the toxic assets, because they cost more than the average and the costs escalate over time.

The scale of mass incarceration has rendered California far more vulnerable to a prison health care crisis than it was in the past. California's obsession with security and custody led to prison siting and design that has greatly increased the cost of supplying adequate health care. Prisons were deliberately built hundreds of miles away from the major coastal cities, mostly in the Central Valley, in mountainous portions of the northern and eastern parts of the state, and on the far northern coastline, locations where health care professionals are in very short supply. Any effort to recruit a professional workforce to such locations (essential to the remedy plan that California agreed to) requires a substantial premium over the salaries in more desirable parts of the state.

Three years into the implementation of Judge Henderson's receivership order, 80 percent of the positions the Department had created in the health system management field were vacant, and "many of the [prison] physicians have prior criminal charges, have had privileges revoked from hospitals, or have mental health problems."[15] The court estimated in 2005 that the California Department of Corrections and Rehabilitation needed to hire at least 150 physicians to fill vacancies and replace manifestly incompetent medical staff. At some institutions, vacancy rates for nurses and medical technical assistants were as high as 80 and 70 percent, respectively.

Most of the *Plata* plaintiffs suffered not from the infectious diseases that have threatened confined populations as long as prisons have existed, nor from gross injuries caused by violent assaults, but from chronic illnesses and long-term physical disabilities. The health challenge posed by chronic illness and disability is that care must be delivered continuously and the patient must be regularly monitored to see if the prescribed treatment needs adjusting. Both require the full cooperation of the patient. If any of these elements falters, the conditions are likely to get worse in ways that make further treatment more difficult, more expensive, and less effective.

In his opinion ordering a receivership, Judge Henderson highlighted dispensing prescriptions to the chronically ill as a crucial failing of the California prison health system. "A sizable portion of CDCR prisoners suffer from chronic illness, yet defendants have failed to devise and implement a system to track and treat these patients, and such patients suffer from a lack of continuity of care."[16]

Chronic diseases are becoming a more important overall problem of health care in the United States and other societies undergoing demographic aging, but California's mass-incarceration policies have concentrated those problems even more intensively in the prison sector. Chronic diseases are often rooted in the lifestyle choices that go along with criminality and frequent imprisonments, including injection drug use, unsafe sex, and lack of access to health care in the community, which can result in diseases such as hepatitis or in damage to the major organs, including the liver or kidneys. These problems are compounded by a prison life that is far more sedentary than it may have been in the past, which leads to other chronic diseases of the heart, lungs, and kidneys, including diabetes and cancer.

From a medical-management perspective, the prison regime is even more problematic for combating chronic disease than infectious disease; a very different set of strategies and technologies are necessary to combat chronic disease. When infectious disease responds to medicine, treating it is fairly cheap; antibiotics and better hygiene don't cost much. Chronic disease, in contrast, starts off expensive; treatment is labor intensive and difficult to automate. Then as a chronic illness advances, treatment costs more and is needed more often.[17]

Because of the cost curves of chronic illness, the only sustainable economic model requires meticulous management of routine care needs. Diabetics, for example, need to measure their blood sugar throughout the day, adjusting their food intake and maybe their insulin. Failure to provide that kind of management results in escalating damage to the kidneys, and degrading kidney function brings damage to the circulatory system, manifested in heart disease and damage to hands and feet. Eventually, in an advanced stage of the disease, kidney dialysis and limb amputations may become necessary, requiring specialists and generating extraordinary costs. The same pattern exists with other chronic diseases, including heart disease, HIV infection, and some cancers. Institutions obligated to finance such care can save enormously by investing in improved routine management and frequent low-cost interventions. Those that do not will face brutally escalating costs.

Mass incarceration's inability to track prisoners individually in real time is an inherent flaw underscored by the *Plata* case. Prisons have always reflected designers' fantasies of totalitarian surveillance and control, but the reality has often been far less rigorous. Prisons built in the last decades of the twentieth century in the richest state in the nation, home to the technology industry and with a highly centralized bureaucratic prison system, should have come closer than most to achieving the historic dream of individualized knowledge of the prisoner and an ability to act on that knowledge beneficially. But even before chronic hyper-overcrowding began to make California's mass-incarceration prisons totally dysfunctional, their layout and procedures prevented prison officials thinking about or treating their prisoners as individuals.

This disregard was epitomized by total failure to maintain

medical records and scheduling systems. Modern medicine is built on records. Except in an emergency, medical care given without reviewing a person's medical records constitutes malpractice almost by definition. With chronic illnesses, the need for long-term, frequently adjusted treatments requires a routinized capacity to maintain medical records and to provide regular scheduling and follow-up for multiple medical appointments. Without these routines, small problems aggregate into catastrophes, and medical treatment itself becomes a risk to life and limb. For the *Plata* plaintiffs, referrals to specialists or specialty diagnostic tools (like MRIs) were regularly lost, ignored, or repeated, leaving months or even years between the identification of a serious condition and medical confirmation, with even more delays before approved treatments were performed. As the *Plata* receivership opinion and order chronicles,

> The amount of unfiled, disorganized, and literally unusable medical records paperwork at some prisons is staggering. (Three and one-half feet of loose filing at San Quentin in December 2004) . . . (twelve to eighteen inches of loose filing at Salinas Valley in January 2005); and (six to eight feet of loose filing at CSP-Sacramento in January 2005). At CIM, the records were kept in a 30 foot long trailer with no light except for a small hole cut into the roof and were arranged into piles without any apparent order.[18]

The *Plata* case revealed the huge disconnect between mass incarceration and the ethos of caregiving. Under mass incarceration, prison officers and managers have come to view medical care as alien—subversive of total incapacitation. Even the most basic medical efforts—examinations, appointment confirmations, pharmacy access for medications, follow-up—already grossly inadequate due to the lack of health care infrastructure, were viewed with disdain. Custodial officers were routinely hostile to medical providers, and they treated prisoners' medical complaints as impositions, a tactic in the ongoing war and an opportunity to retaliate.[19]

The administrators who aggressively sought to control every instant of the lives of more people for longer periods just as aggressively rejected any responsibility to care for these people's health. As undersecretary of corrections Kevin Carruth, testifying before the court at the hearing on the receivership, bluntly explained to Judge Henderson, "Medical care is not a priority within CDCR, is not considered a 'core competency' of the Department, and is not the business of the CDC[R], and it will never be the business of the Department of Corrections to provide medical care."[20]

Judge Henderson's appointment of a receiver amounted to a public finding that California cannot give constitutional medical care to its prison population because its officials don't care and can't even imagine caring. As his opinion notes, "The prison is unable to function effectively and suffers a lack of will with respect to prisoner medical care." California's prison leadership was not just incompetent at medical care; it had established a penal logic antithetical to it. This leadership gap runs through all the other problems confronting health care delivery in California's prisons and was the factor most critical in requiring a receiver, as Judge Henderson further notes:

> Beyond the obvious problem of condoning malpractice and allowing incompetent doctors to remain on staff, the leadership vacuum and lack of discipline also fosters a culture of non-accountability and non-professionalism whereby "the acceptance of degrading and humiliating conditions [becomes] routine and permissible."[21]

Previously, when rehabilitation was a major goal, prison officers shared the operation of the prison with others, including rehabilitation professionals and medical and mental health professionals. When the prison population swelled and incapacitation replaced rehabilitation, the prisons dispensed with professional help and fostered unconstitutional conditions in California prisons.

The *Plata* evidence documents systematic hostility of correctional officers to medical treatment for prisoners and to those who provide it. Prisoners with a medical problem face a formidable gauntlet of prison officers who presume any medical complaint is a scam; ignore visible signs of disease; and refuse to allow exams, treatments, or follow-up. Because doctors have a professional ethical obligation to protect and help their patients regardless of the patients' moral or legal standing, the very nature of prison doctors' work brings them into value conflict with the prevailing prison order. It is assumed that all prisoners are constantly looking for opportunities to assault officers or other inmates and that any variation from a pure custodial regime is a potential breach of security. Of California prisons in the era of mass incarceration, Henderson concludes that "there is a common lack of respect for medical staff, and custody staff far too often actively interfere with the provision of medical care, often for reasons that appear to have nothing or little to do with legitimate custody concerns."[22]

As a result, California prisons hire medical staff who will base their decisions on custodial edict rather than the medical standard of practice. Even when prisoners finally managed to navigate into the presence of an actual physician or nurse, they encountered a medically trained adjunct of the prison, as callous as the prison officers.[23] Testimony in the *Plata* case illustrates this heartlessness in shocking detail:

> In one instance, a prisoner reported a two to three week history of fever and chills and requested care. The prisoner repeatedly visited medical staff with an increasingly serious

heart condition but was consistently sent back to his housing unit. Eventually, the patient received a correct diagnosis
of endocarditis, a potentially fatal heart condition treatable
with antibiotics, but did not get appropriate medication. Finally, the prisoner went to the prison emergency room with
very low blood pressure, a high fever and cyanotic (blue) fin-
gertips, indications of seriously deficient blood flow and
probable shock. Despite the objections of a nurse who recognized the severity of the prisoner's condition, the physician
attempted to return the patient to his housing unit without
treatment. Rather than being sent to a community hospital
emergency room for immediate treatment, as would have
been appropriate, the patient was sent to the prison's Out-
patient Housing Unit for observation. He died shortly there-
after from cardiac arrest.[24]

In another case:

[A] prisoner repeatedly requested to see a doctor regarding acute abdominal and chest pains; the triage nurse can-
celed the medical appointment, thinking the prisoner was
faking illness. When the prisoner requested transfer to another prison for treatment, his doctor refused the request
without conducting an examination. A doctor did see the
prisoner a few weeks later but refused to examine him because the prisoner had arrived with a self-diagnosis and
the doctor found this unacceptable. The prisoner died two
weeks later.[25]

And in yet another example:

[A] San Quentin prisoner with hypertension, diabetes and
renal failure was prescribed two different medications that
actually served to exacerbate his renal failure. An optome-

trist noted the patient's retinal bleeding due to very high blood pressure and referred him for immediate evaluation, but this evaluation never took place. It was not until a year later that the patient's renal failure was recognized, at which point he was referred to a nephrologist on an urgent basis; he should have been seen by a specialist within 14 days but the consultation never happened and the patient died three months later. Dr. Puisis testified that "it was like watching the natural history of blood pressure turn into chronic renal failure somewhat similar to the Tuskegee experiment."[26]

Unlike the examples of savage violence captured in earlier cases (including *Madrid*), these examples of cruelty through deliberate indifference to serious health care needs cannot be easily assigned to individual wrongdoers. They describe instead a systematic, planned method of running a large-scale institution designed to degrade people and encourage inhumane conduct toward them.

*   *   *

The *Plata* receivership order and opinion may mark the revival of medical expertise and values in the prisons of mass incarceration from which they had been expelled by California's extreme total-incapacitation penal philosophy. The thirty-year experiment with mass incarceration was a break with tradition. Medical care had been considered important in California prisons in the nineteenth and most of the twentieth centuries, and this attitude had its origins in American correctional ideas going back to the time of the Revolution and lasting through several shifts in medical and penal standards.

In 1777, John Howard, a minor English nobleman and justice of the peace, published a book condemning health conditions in the jails of Britain and Europe that helped mobilize support for a long wave of penal reform in the Atlantic world (a movement that remains incomplete today). *The State of the Prisons in England and Wales* was a detailed catalog of conditions and inmate populations in jails throughout those countries that played a role similar to that of contemporary correctional statistics.[27] At the same time, Howard's book was among the most forceful moral polemics of the age, confronting its elite readers with the moral and scientific fact that jails condemned all sorts of people, including innocents wrongly held and those not imprisoned, to untimely deaths through exposure to "jail diseases."

Typhus, smallpox, and yellow fever regularly killed prisoners in large numbers, but these diseases also claimed the lives of judges, barristers, and elite citizens who watched trials in the courts. Other diseases also flared into outbreaks that might threaten whole urban populations. In the prevailing medical ideas of the age, these diseases were caused by the vapors thought to arise from decomposing organic matter. Breathing in these vapors, over time, was believed to give rise to illness. Treatment and prevention required cleansing the environment and removing infected individuals from exposure to impure air.

Howard's condemnation of the unhealthy conditions in local jails lay behind the prison reform movement that swept the Atlantic world.[28] Howard designed prisons that would be easily cleansed and would prevent the spread of contamination by ventilation and by separation of inmates for sleep.[29] Howard extended the miasma-medicine model to crime, believing that criminality could be reversed by separating offenders from corrupting, crime-inducing influences in a well-disciplined, well-designed prison.

Howard's cause was taken up in the United States by Benjamin Rush, a Philadelphia physician and one of the penitentiary's major proponents in the early Republic.[30] In England a decade after Howard's book, Jeremy Bentham, the influential political philosopher often considered the founder of the utilitarian tradition, promoted his own plan for a penitentiary in a pamphlet published as *Panopticon; or, The Inspection House*. Bentham's pamphlet underlined the centrality of health among the variety of possible goals of the prison.[31]

> A Penitentiary-house, more particularly is . . . what every prison might, and in some degree at least ought to be, designed at once as a place of safe custody, and a place of labour. Every such place must necessarily be, whether designed or not, an hospital—a place where sickness will be found at least, whether provision be or be not made for its relief.[32]

The link between the threat of disease and prisons, as well as the promise of medical methods and treatments to prevent crime, inspired continuing efforts to reshape the prison, all of which emphasized the importance of medical expertise. New medical models of crime developed in the late nineteenth and twentieth centuries, producing profound changes in penal strategy and practices. Eugenics emphasized the function of prisons in removing those biologically disposed to crime from the reproductive population, and psychotherapy emphasized the role of prisons in diagnosing the complex of factors leading individuals into crime and in providing appropriate therapies.

The ambitious promises of a medical model for prisons that would successfully treat crime through humane individualized care, which was especially prominent after World War II, were belied by persistent complaints about disease and extremely poor health care in prisons. Even where medical care was at its best, as in the advanced progressive states such as California, prison medicine was closely tied to the punitive control function, leading to unethical experiments and cruel use of medical treatment as a bargaining chip to control prisoners. Despite that, when federal courts in the 1960s and 1970s began to develop the meaning of the Constitution's ban on cruel and unusual punishment for prison conditions,[33] the Supreme Court held that a right to necessary health care in prison was a core part of that promise.[34] During this period, medical and correctional professionals collaborated on standards for prison health care to forestall violations of that promise.[35]

Thus as California and other states began the great prison boom of the 1980s, the framework for maintaining health in prison seemed secure, backed up by two centuries of correctional philosophy and two decades of court decisions and correctional standard-setting. The *Plata* case revealed how rapidly and dramatically that security had disintegrated, even in the richest state in the nation, one with a history of medical ambition in prisons. By gathering a population of chronically ill people, many of them serving long sentences, in prisons that had lost the capacity to know and act on their inmates as individuals, mass incarceration created a humanitarian crisis not unlike the one that Howard described 250 years ago.

*   *   *

The *Plata* receivership decision also marked a significant change in the tone of the judicial process. *Madrid* and *Coleman* had exposed terrible and systematic failures, but they retained the legitimating presumption that the state and CDCR were still engaged in the "unenviable" task of holding "dangerous men in safe custody under humane conditions."[36] Judge Henderson recognized that he was dealing with an organized system of inhumanity.

In its depiction of suffering and its sense of urgency for the imprisoned, the *Plata* receivership order also marks a change in the image of the prisoner. *Plata* represents prisoners as a population at risk of death or severe suffering as a direct result of incarceration. From a population defined primarily by the risks they pose to others, prisoners had been reframed as a population themselves at risk. As the *Plata* case moved into a receivership phase, the litigation reached beyond prison conditions to address policy choices far larger than even the sweeping reform agenda set forth in the stipulated agreement that originally resolved the case in 2002. Judge Henderson writes, "Decades of neglecting medical care while vastly increasing the size of the prison population has led to a state of institutional paralysis." Writing of what he termed "the problem of Democratic Debilitation," Judge Henderson frames the receivership order as a necessary response to a crisis of political institutions:

> To a significant extent, this case presents a textbook example of how majoritarian political institutions sometimes fail to muster the will to protect a disenfranchised, stigmatized, and unpopular subgroup of the population. The failure of political will, combined with a massive escalation in the rate of incarceration over the past few decades, has led to a serious and chronic abnegation of the State responsibility for the basic medical needs of prisoners. This is a case where "the failure of the political bodies is so egregious and the demands for protection of constitutional rights so importunate that there is no practical alternative to federal court intervention." [Citation omitted.][37]

With the receivership order, litigation had begun for the first time to define mass incarceration as the source of unconstitutional conditions in California's prisons.

Judge Henderson blamed California's crisis squarely on a set of public policies that increased the prison infrastructure and population without creating a managerial capacity to look after the internal needs of such a large and medically needy population.[38] It was no longer a question of whether Marciano Plata or other individual prisoner plaintiffs had been tortured by their lack of adequate medical treatment; it was the systematic risks of accumulating injury inflicted on California's prisoners—torture on the installment plan—that now stood condemned. California built prisons without taking the humanity of prisoners into account. The Eighth Amendment required that these prisons be fixed. In 2005 with his receivership order, the judge went as far as he could to separate that remedy from the existing dysfunctional bureaucracy of California's prisons by placing implementation in the hands of a fully independent actor with all of the extraordinary powers of the federal courts. If that was not sufficient to bring the unconstitutional abuse to an end, the next step would have to question the constitutionality of the very policies of mass imprisonment.

5

Places of Extreme Peril

Coleman-Plata v. Schwarzenegger *and California's*
Prisons in the Era of Chronic Hyper-Overcrowding

Tough-on-crime politics have increased the population of California's prisons dramatically while making necessary reforms
impossible. As a result, the state's prisons have become places
"of extreme peril to the safety of persons" they house, while
contributing little to the safety of California's residents. . . .
— *Coleman-Plata v. Schwarzenegger,* Three-Judge Court,
Final Order and Opinion, August 2009[1]

Judge Henderson's receivership order in the *Plata* case should
have shaken the foundations of California's political and legal
establishment to its foundations. Instead, it marked the high
tide of accountability on the part of the State. Having failed to
acknowledge that anything was wrong despite the court ruling, California's defendant officials made empty promises. In
late 2006, a year after the receivership order in *Plata* placed
prisoner medical treatment under direct court control and
eleven years after the *Coleman* decision ordered reform of prison
mental health care, lawyers for the prisoners in both cases returned to their respective courts and asked their judges to
strengthen previous orders and impose a population cap as a

way of relieving chronic extreme overcrowding. Without such reform, it was felt, the promise to repair an unconstitutionally defective medical care system for prisoners, unfilled for more than a decade, might never be kept. In August 2009, some months after the trial, the special three-judge court issued the largest prison injunction order in history. The opinion accompanying the order painted a radical portrait of mass incarceration at its most pathological.

Rarely if ever has a federal court so directly called into question a state's penal policies. Even more remarkable, in an era of extreme deference by courts to state governments, especially on the topic of criminal justice, the court challenged the central rationale of four decades of mass incarceration in the United States. Instead of protecting the public by keeping dangerous men secure in humane conditions, the largest, most expensive prison system in the country had actually decreased public safety by keeping them in "extreme peril" under inhumane conditions.

The *Coleman-Plata* decision allows us to understand more clearly the last phase of mass incarceration in California, from the mid-1990s through 2009, a period distinguished by an unprecedented chronic hyper-overcrowding that ultimately led to a state of emergency. Although California's overcrowding was uniquely bad, it's an identifying symptom of mass incarceration throughout the country. The decision in *Coleman-Plata* points out a judicial path to ending it.

The *Coleman-Plata* decision considered mass incarceration in a different legal framework. In the *Madrid*, *Coleman*, and *Plata* cases, the legal question was whether or not California was violating the Eighth Amendment ban on cruel and unusual punishment. The population-cap remedy in *Coleman-Plata* was an answer to a different set of questions, not about the constitutional rights of prisoners but about overcrowding and public safety. The court was forced to ask these questions by the

Prison Litigation Reform Act of 1996, passed at the height of mass incarceration with the support of both political parties and the enthusiastic signature of President Bill Clinton. Under this act, before a court could impede a state's freedom to incarcerate more people, the court must directly weigh the potential impact of any population cap or reduction order on public safety.

Mass incarceration was simply supposed to be an expansion of twentieth-century correctional modernism. By 2000, it was clear that something else had emerged. What criminologist Mona Lynch has called "a prototype of postrehabilitative penology" was pioneered in Arizona as no-frills custody built to protect the public as cheaply as possible.[2] In California, this postrehabilitative model took an even more extreme form, as the high costs of building more prisons combined with the imperatives of total incapacitation to create a period of severe overcrowding that lasted for decades and led to a new way of operating prisons characterized by emergency governance, complete loss of individuation, and absence of mobility.

Mass incarceration's target is not the rational actor who must be deterred or the pathological deviant who must be confined and treated, but a whole population of people believed to be permanently committed to a criminal lifestyle. The goal of mass incarceration is to keep as much of this population incapacitated as much of the time as possible. Although there is little evidence for this assumption, mass imprisonment does create a class of people *labeled* as permanently criminal. Yet this huge class has often escaped the attention of courts, which normally deal with the rights of individuals. Even in large class actions, judges generally think in terms of groups of individuals, as in *Madrid, Coleman,* and *Plata.* In *Coleman-Plata,* however, the prison population en masse finally had its day in court.

The three judges in *Coleman-Plata* held a fourteen-day evidentiary hearing. In deference to the Prison Litigation Reform

Art, they focused for thirteen days on the public-safety implications of ordering California to find alternatives to state prison for many of the felons and parole violators routinely imprisoned since the late 1970s. Almost a year later, the court issued its order. Finding that the use of such alternatives for thousands convicted of nonviolent felonies would pose little risk to public safety, the court ordered the State of California to reduce its population by at least forty thousand inmates so that its prisons would be at no more than 137 percent of design capacity within two years.

Mass incarceration was the subject of litigation for the first time. The abstract sociolegal concept became terrifyingly real in California's hyper-overcrowded prisons. *Coleman-Plata* showed that overcrowding was not a temporary exception in prison government but was a *method* of governing prisons by putting them in a perpetual state of emergency. The overcrowding was chronic; it lasted over twenty years. And it was extreme, from 200 percent of design capacity to as high as 300 percent at some prisons. The *Coleman-Plata* decision was the first step toward finding unconstitutional the governing mechanisms necessary to maintain control in massively overcrowded prisons.

Overcrowding has been a perennial problem in the history of prisons. That's because of the gap between those responsible for building and running prisons (usually state officials under direct control of the legislature and the governor) and those responsible for gathering the prisoners (generally local prosecutors, judges, and police, although parole boards and governors help at the back end). Prison officials typically have a hard time persuading their political superiors to approve the high fixed costs of a whole new prison, as opposed to the incremental costs of cramming a few more people into the old ones. Local officials, in contrast, have every incentive to offload their difficult residents to the state prison system, where in most states they will be housed and fed at state expense with no local contribution expected.

In the era of mass incarceration, this gap became a canyon. Prosecutors committed themselves to maximizing the prison population by charging the most serious crimes possible. They put convicts away for longer than ever with an arsenal of new laws featuring mandatory minimum sentences, abolition of parole, and sentence enhancements for use of weapons enacted by state legislators—many of them former prosecutors— eager to show their support for the campaign.[3] State prison operators lost what little control they once had over the release of prisoners, as parole was abolished in many states.[4] Legislatures and governors have consistently backed all manner of sentence enhancements and committed their states to building a host of new bond-funded prisons—but far fewer than necessary to meet the prisoner yield of the laws they had authorized. It was easy to enact harsh new laws under the deterrence theory, but when state revenues were hit by the recession of 2001, most states stopped building new prisons.

California's prisons never caught up with the population influx, and as the prison-building boom ebbed in the 1990s, the population reached a steady norm of about 200 percent of design capacity. By the time the *Coleman-Plata* court was looking at the issue, overcrowding had produced a permanent state of chaos that had its own name—"bad beds."

Thousands of prisoners are assigned to "bad beds," such as triple-bunked beds placed in gymnasiums or day rooms, and some institutions have populations approaching 300% of their intended capacity. In these overcrowded conditions, inmate-on-inmate violence is almost impossible to prevent, infectious diseases spread more easily, and lockdowns are sometimes the only means by which to maintain control. In short, California's prisons are bursting at the seams and are impossible to manage.[5]

These spaces were more like refugee camps or Third World jails than what Americans associate with a modern prison. Moreover, they were not temporary; they have remained for two decades. Tens of thousands of Californians have served their time in these dangerous and degrading circumstances, and a generation of prison officers and prison managers has learned its job in this context. As a result, the chronic hyper-overcrowding has created a distinctive kind of prison order, a form of "emergency government" with no attractive historical precedents.[6]

The 1996 Prison Litigation Reform Act instructs federal courts not to impede a state from taking more prisoners, even to correct unconstitutional conditions, except as a last resort. A court considering a population-reduction order must find, on the record, that the problem it seeks to address—in this instance, overcrowding—is the primary cause of the unconstitutional condition and that no other reasonable means are available to rectify it. To determine whether those conditions were met in California, the *Coleman-Plata* court had to examine closely the way overcrowding interacted with the fundamental failures of mental and medical health care exposed in the earlier cases. The court found that the very possibility of establishing regular and routine health care was made remote by the sustained state of hyper-overcrowding in California's prisons.

The court identified the perpetual state of emergency as a specific feature of overcrowding that precluded a constitutionally acceptable level of health care.[7] Prisons have always operated in the shadow of emergency. Their mission—to confine those deemed criminal threats—means that a breakdown of internal control (such as a riot) or a breach of the security of the prison's exterior (such as an escape) is a scandal of significance at the highest levels of state government. A prison emergency, whatever its nature, results in an intensification of discipline and control to the point of a complete shutdown of all other operations of the prison until the danger has been ended. Such emergencies have almost always resulted in changes of leadership, if not a crisis of legitimacy. What makes California distinctive in the era of chronic hyper-overcrowding is the degree to which emergency government became a routine feature that *did not* threaten the careers of bureaucrats or the legitimacy of the prison system. The harsh discipline and in-cell control that followed emergencies in the past now became a permanent mode of administration.

Even at normal capacity, large prisons often would have to invoke emergency procedures due to the difficulty of moving selected people within large populations. But as prison populations exceeded 200 percent of design capacity, the result was a continual state of emergency. One of the plaintiff's prison experts, a former manager of Texas's sprawling prison system, described the way this operated at the level of individual prisons:

> Overcrowding has burdened CDCR's [California Department of Corrections and Rehabilitation] inadequate management systems that underlie health care delivery. The excessive population leads to management failures in two ways. First, overcrowding engenders a state of perpetual crisis that causes management failures. Administrators spend their time doing damage control, rather than making sure the prison is operating properly and prisoners are getting the services that they need. . . . A population of 7,000 or more, as is found in some California prisons, is not manageable at all. The sheer size and complexities of managing a prison that size would be overwhelming for one manager especially with the limited resources in the areas of staffing and

inadequate space for services to the offenders that I observed
at all of the prisons I toured in California. One warden simply cannot know what he/she needs to know on a daily basis
to make good informed management decisions.[8]

One of California's major proposals to solve the overcrowding problem without a population cap was to enlarge existing
prisons by building more housing units. One of the plaintiff's
experts, former California secretary of corrections Jean Woodford, explained why that would only add to the system's permanent state of crisis:

> The so-called "in-fill" beds will cause more problems than
> they will solve. Many of California's prisons are so big that
> they are effectively unmanageable. Wardens and other ad-
> ministrators spend much of their time responding to cri-
> ses, rather than fulfilling their responsibilities to provide
> adequate medical and mental health care. Unless these in-
> fill beds stand alone with their own administrative and
> support facilities, adding thousands of additional prison-
> ers to already overburdened facilities will only compound
> the burdens imposed on prison administrators and line
> staff.[9]

Emergency mode was in effect at the top levels of the system,
as well as the bottom. State prison officials addressed the problem with ad hoc tactics including moving prisoners around the
state in a kind of three-card monte game. The depth of the dif-
ficulties was illustrated dramatically in 2006, on the eve of the
Coleman-Plata case, when then-governor Arnold Schwarzenegger declared a state of emergency in the prison system. The
terms used in the emergency declaration were not those of
public exposure to crime, but of prisons as sites of danger and
disease. In their opinion, the three-judge court took the gover-

nor's declaration as an important piece of evidence of the failure of reform:

> In his Prison Overcrowding State of Emergency Proclamation, the Governor declared that . . . "the severe overcrowding in 29 CDCR prisons has caused substantial risk to the health and safety of the men and women who work inside these prisons and the inmates housed in them"; that "the overcrowding crisis gets worse with each passing day, creating an emergency in the California prison system"; and that "immediate action is necessary to prevent death and harm caused by California's severe prison overcrowding." . . .
> The risks enumerated by the Governor in his Proclamation include "increased, substantial risk for transmission of infectious illness"; security risks caused by line-of-sight problems for correctional officers, particularly in areas where inmates are triple-bunked and in "tight quarters"; and "thousands of gallons of sewage spills and environmental contamination" from overloading the prisons' sewage and wastewater systems. . . . Governor Schwarzenegger also declared that the suicide rate in the 29 severely overcrowded prisons "[was] approaching an average of one per week."[10]

One result of emergency government was the gradual transformation of prisons into giant blocks of immobility. Obviously, prisons imply immobility; they are designed to fix the location of individuals whose punishment consists largely of exile from the community. However, after the early disaster of total solitary confinement in the Jacksonian-era penitentiaries, American prisons depended on strategies to organize and mobilize prisoners. For much of the nineteenth and twentieth centuries, industrial or agricultural labor was the primary instrument of mobility in prisons. In the North, the Big House prisons consisted of housing blocks and adjoining

workshops. Prisons used their prisoners as slave labor in me-
nial manufacturing work, putting some of the money from the
work contracts into minimal food and upkeep. Mobility consisted of marching prisoners from cells to shops and back
again. In the South, African American prisoners rarely saw the
inside of a public prison but were enslaved on-site at the work-
place. After World War II, as the idea of providing therapy and
education took hold, prisons were redesigned to function more
like large high schools or colleges, with dormitories linked by
hallways to educational and service buildings.

While American corrections has generated very different
approaches to governing prisoners, almost all of them (at
least the ones that have avoided humanitarian disrepute)
found ways to mobilize prisoners in their own, or more often
someone else's, activities. Mass incarceration, with its commitment to simply storing as many people as possible, is an
exception.

Mass incarceration favors immobility, and overcrowding
worsens it. It's at its worst in the supermax, where prisoners
are locked in their cells twenty-three hours a day with no work
assignments or programs of any kind. Even meals are "served"
in-cell. Inmates of California's lower-security prisons are supposed to spend most of their days outside the cell, but overcrowding has led to frequent lockdowns, preventing any
semblance of normal schedules, while the removal of educational or recreational programs leaves fewer possible activities
in any case. Under lockdown, prisoners remain in their cells all
day. Those in the "bad beds" packed into irregular prison places
spend all day sitting on a tiny bunk or standing in the crowded
temporary spaces between bunks. *Coleman-Plata* found:

> All inmates must spend increasingly larger chunks of their
> days in their cells, or much more dangerously, in one of
> those triple-bunked "non-traditional" spaces. None of this

is conducive to the health and well-being of any inmate, much less a seriously mentally disordered inmate/patient.[11]

Staggering from emergency to emergency and relying more and more on total immobilization, California prison managers came to treat prisoners not as individuals but as a mass that posed such a threat that it could not be differentiated or individualized. The classic example of such a mass is an invading enemy army, which is organized and disciplined to act as a collective unit and must be lethally addressed as a whole. Outside of riot situations and the convict-lease system for African American prisoners in the post–Civil War South, American prisoners generally have not been treated this way. Under mass incarceration, however, prisoners are known and acted upon only as an enemy population.

For the court in *Coleman-Plata*, this approach manifested itself primarily in the way overcrowding prevented the state from establishing constitutional levels of mental health and medical care. While the state stressed (and still stresses) the overall amount of money it has spent improving medical infrastructures and staffing, overcrowding meant that prisoners as individuals were inevitably lost. For example, prisoners with serious mental illnesses entering prison reception centers for the first time, or again on a parole violation, never received mental health screening and so spent their entire prison sentences in a "bad bed" without the medication necessary to prevent their illness from worsening. And this was the case more than a decade after the courts had found California prisons unconstitutional for not providing just such screening and treatment.

Overcrowding had become the engine of failure and suffering in the California prison system. Overcrowding made efforts at building a new infrastructure for health care delivery and hiring new professional staff largely futile, and became a routinized framework in which both prisoners and prison officers operated. Experts for the plaintiffs argued that hyper-overcrowding was at the root of the security-obsessed culture among correctional workers, as argued in *Coleman*:

> Dr. Beard testified, a culture that allows "custodial interference with the delivery of care" is problematic, but "you have to realize that the culture grew out of the overcrowding." . . . Crowded conditions force prison administrators "to take a strong custodial approach. . . . They have to rely on the lock-downs. They have to rely on guns, gas, those kinds of things, to control the prisons so they're safe for the staff and for their inmates."[12]

The court found by clear and convincing evidence that ending the overcrowding was essential to any hope of realizing the other constitutional goals:

> Crowding of reception centers at levels approaching 300% design capacity prevents the state from identifying the medical problems of entering inmates, and makes it impossible to provide necessary medical and mental health care to incoming inmates, who routinely remain in reception centers for more than sixty days and may serve their entire sentence there. Crowding has also left the California prison system without the space, beds, and medical, mental health, and custodial staff required to provide constitutionally adequate medical and mental health care in all parts of the prison system, and has prevented proper classification of inmates and appropriate housing according to their needs. Furthermore, crowding has created conditions of confinement that contribute to the spread of disease, and it requires the increased use of lockdowns as a method of prison control, further impeding the prison authorities' ability to provide needed

medical and mental health care. In addition, crowding has prevented the development of an adequate medical records system. The consequences of crowding are often dangerous, and on many occasions fatal. Crowding contributes to an alarming number of extreme departures from the standard of care and an unacceptably high number of inmate deaths that are preventable or possibly preventable. Likewise, crowding worsens many of the risk factors for suicide among California inmates and increases the prevalence and acuity of mental illness throughout the prison system.[13]

The court found that any hope of changing the culture of hostility toward medical treatment for prisoners required an end to the permanent overcrowding:

> Thus, although we agree with Dr. Thomas that a custody-dominated culture is a barrier to delivering constitutionally adequate care, we also agree with Dr. Beard that "[i]f you try to change the culture, you can't. You can't change the culture until you reduce the population and can make the institution safe." . . . Consequently, it is crowding and not culture that is the primary cause of the unconstitutional system of health care delivery in California's prisons.[14]

The state of California had *planned* its prisons to be overcrowded, designing infrastructure for water and sewage to operate at 190 percent of capacity while providing for medical and mental health care not even at a normal occupancy level. Under mass incarceration, overcrowding has become a normal feature of imprisonment nationwide; more than half of the states had prison populations well in excess of design capacity in 2010. Although none has created a humanitarian crisis as large and shocking as California's, the threat of torturelike conditions for prisoners with chronic illness is all too real in most states.[15] This system and its resulting damages must be recognized for what it was (and perhaps still is): the greatest domestic human rights violation committed by a state government outside the South under slavery and segregation.

Ironically, the three-judge court's confrontation with total incapacitation was precipitated in part by the Prison Litigation Reform Act, which required the court to give substantial weight to the impact of any prisoner release on public safety. Compelled to address the issue of public safety squarely, the three judges had no choice but to challenge the incapacitative common sense head-on.

The act reflected a canard popular among politicians in the 1990s—that federal courts had become a vehicle for frivolous attacks by prisoners and civil rights lawyers on state prisons, and that federal judges were elitists hostile to the moral purposes of punishment and indifferent to the dangers posed by actual prisoners. As a result, the act provides a veritable armory of tools that state prison systems and their allies—prosecutors, probation officers, sheriffs, and police chiefs—can use to combat prisoner lawsuits and court remedies.

The Reform Act sets the very highest hurdles for any kind of court-ordered prison reforms or constraints on the size of prison populations. This aspect of the law testifies to the importance that the highest levels of political authority placed on removing any legal obstacles to maximizing the state prison population.[16] The law requires that a population cap be adopted by a special federal court with three judges, including at least one judge from the court of appeals.[17] The public safety issue was particularly charged in Coleman-Plata because, more than any other state, California has committed itself to the view that state prison is the only reliable way to prevent convicted felons from committing more crimes. This "common sense" assumes that all convicts, regardless of their crimes or life histories, pose an unacceptably high risk of committing serious violent crimes in the future.

In considering a population cap for California prisons, the three-judge court was compelled to confront directly this extreme commitment to incapacitation. The court explicitly accepted the argument that locking up enormous numbers of people reduces crime rates: "We acknowledge the concern of some law enforcement officials that incarceration serves the interest of incapacitation over the life of a repeat offender. To that extent, there is likely some correlation between incarceration rates and crime rates."[18] Nonetheless, the court found that the population reduction it was considering was unlikely to undermine public safety because of the state's ability to achieve that reduction through early release or nonimprisonment of very low-risk individuals.

Advocates of mass incarceration tend to focus on aggregate incarceration and aggregate crime rates. Their premise that a higher incarceration rate leads to a crime rate lower than it would otherwise have been presumes that prisoners would be actively committing crimes if they were back in the community. By the same reasoning, locking everybody up would reduce crime to zero. But the key metric in a crime-reduction strategy is the *marginal incapacitative effect*, that is, the additional crime-control value obtained by imprisoning the person who is right on the edge of incarceration under existing policies.[19] The very size of California's prisoner population means that this marginal inmate, who would not be in prison under even slightly less restrictive policies, is likely to pose very little risk of committing a serious and/or violent crime.[20] Noting that other states had reduced prison populations without increasing crime by adopting measures comparable to those proposed by the expert witnesses, the court asserted that California "could [reduce its prison population] perhaps more easily" precisely because its "unproductive incarceration policies" included so many prisoners whose risk of future serious crime is extremely low. Not coincidentally, the prisoners facing serous medical and mental health problems who formed the two constituent classes of the litigation provided numerous examples of prisoners who posed very little risk of committing crime in the future.

This conclusion removes one of the most durable legs on which total incapacitation stands: the presumption that if some time in prison reduces crime, more time will reduce it further in a continuous and linear fashion. California's determinate sentencing system was not enacted to create a system of mass incarceration for incapacitative purposes but rather to deter crime and produce justice by delivering punishment proportionate to the crime in ways transparent to both the victim and the criminal. But beginning in the 1980s, the sentencing system was transformed into an incapacitative system, not as a result of a systematic overhaul of the penal code, but by many individual laws lengthening prison terms in general and specifically for factors like guns and repeat offenses. As a result, prison sentences in California have little or no relationship to justice for the actual crime committed or the risk of future crime. The court rejected the basic premise of danger behind California prisoners with unprecedented bluntness:

> Sentencing judges and prison authorities have little ability to ensure that sentences and conditions of incarceration reflect the circumstances of a particular crime and offender. Similarly, characteristics suggesting that the offender presents a low risk of recidivism or would more effectively serve his sentence in a correctional setting besides prison, including the fact that the offender is elderly or infirm, cannot be considered.[21]

The weight of the evidence showed that, because length of stay is unrelated to recidivism, all else being equal the

likelihood that a person who is released a few months before his original release date will reoffend is the same as if
he were released on his original release date.[22]

For years the state's political leaders have ominously warned
against the danger posed by "early release" of inmates at the
behest of judges or parole authorities, conveniently ignoring
the fact that the state releases nearly a hundred thousand convicted felons a year at the expiration of their determinate sentences without any basis for believing that they will not pose a
danger to the public. Because California prison sentences are
based on the crime and not on individual risk assessment or
rehabilitation (as they were in the era of indeterminate sentences), whether prisoners serve every month of their sentences
or not matters very little for their likelihood of reoffending
once back in the community.

The evidence presented to the court suggested that any abstract incapacitation gains were likely wiped out by the crimi-
nogenic effects of being confined in conditions of chronic
hyper-overcrowding. The most compelling examples were prisoners living with a serious mental illness. As the *Coleman-Plata*
opinion documented:

> [D]efendants' mental health expert reported that mentally
> ill individuals "often enter the prison system with a more
> acute mental health presentation, not having received ade-
> quate treatment in the community and/or having abused
> substances there." . . . These inmates are "disproportion-
> ately represented" among the parole violators returning to
> custody for short sentences . . . and are thus likely to spend
> their entire sentence at the reception center. . . . Because their
> sentences are so short, they are frequently discharged before
> receiving treatment and fall into "a vicious cycle, as they
> decompensate in the community and quickly return. . . ."

"[M]entally ill parolees often do not receive meaningful mental health treatment when they are on parole. . . . Frequently as a result of their decompensation, many are returned to prison, often for technical or minor violations. Thus, many of the parole violations that return them to prison are directly related to their unmet mental health needs."[23]

California's penal philosophy was set in the traumatic days following the San Quentin prison takeover of 1971. It was nurtured on images of prisoners as violent revolutionaries (or terrorists, in today's terms) and presumed an unchanging high level of threat that could be reduced only by physical isolation. This ideology has proven remarkably impervious to critique. If a prisoner is released and commits another crime, incapacitation has not failed, because it presupposes that prisoners pose a high and unchanging risk. It also presupposes that while in prison, these risks do not get worse—that is, no amount of deprivation and brutalization in prison will increase the risk of another crime when the prisoner gets out. So long as both suppositions appear to be common sense, mass incarceration enjoys a certain legitimacy despite its many public problems, including high costs and extreme levels of recidivism.[24]

This faulty logic has proved to be an impenetrable barrier to political efforts to reform mass incarceration in California. Any program that would send fewer people to prison or result in their leaving prison earlier runs into the fatal presumption that it inevitably raises the risks of crime for ordinary citizens. Many of the three-judge court's recommendations for safe ways to reduce the California prison population have been repeatedly made since the mid-1980s, but they have crashed on the shoals of this common sense.[25] Courts often merely reproduce the mistakes of their times, but on occasion their fact-finding power allows the formation of a clearer picture.

The *Coleman-Plata* court's Final Opinion and Order show-cased a large body of criminological research on alternatives to imprisonment and on improved reentry management. Most of those experts presented by the plaintiffs were nationally prom-inent social scientists based in California, including leading criminologists, such as Barry Krisberg and Joan Petersilia, and psychologists, such as Craig Haney. Indeed, many of them had advised the state in commissioned reports on how to rebalance the tilt toward incarceration, but time and again nothing had happened.[26]

Starting with what they considered the least controversial changes to California's mass-incarceration policies, the court recommended three different strategies for diverting the flow that had sustained California's mammoth prison population for a generation.

First, the court recommended that the state introduce cred-its to prisoners who complete rehabilitative programs that have shown effectiveness in reducing recidivism.

Second, the court recommended that California risk-assess and divert many parole violators to alternative programs or sanctions rather than returning them to prison. In California all of the nearly hundred thousand men and women leaving prison every year face an additional three years of reporting to a state parole officer and complying with a set of conditions enforced by that officer. Nearly seventy thousand California parolees were returned to prison on a parole violation (as op-posed to a conviction for a new crime) in 2009, the year of the *Coleman-Plata* decision.

Parole violators, whose short sentences (capped by statute at twelve months, with an average of four) rarely last long enough to process them through reception under conditions of chronic hyper-overcrowding, had long been the biggest source of prison admissions in California and one with the least credible public-safety benefit. Indeed, the court quoted defense expert Joan Petersilia's alarming image of parolee imprisonment as a "catch and release" policy that "is creating a destructive situation by constantly cycling offenders in and out of prison and their home communities in a way that blurs the distinction between the two and combines the worst elements of each."[27]

Third, the court recommended diverting many of the men and women convicted of very low-level felonies to alternative sanctions in the community, again based on risk assessment. In conjunction with this, the court also recommended reviving a "probation subsidy" program that California used in the 1960s to reward counties that kept people convicted of minor felonies in the community on probation.

The State of California formally abandoned rehabilitation as a rationale for punishment in the 1976 Determinate Sentence Law and largely abandoned rehabilitative programs in the 1980s. In 2003, Governor Arnold Schwarzenegger revived the idea that prisons should rehabilitate, changing the name of the prison bureau to the Department of Corrections and Rehabilitation. Yet at the time of the litigation, few rehabilitation programs were available, and many of them came from volunteers. The court recommended actually implementing some programs shown to reduce recidivism. In contrast to the 1970s, when California's political class accepted a highly pessimistic penology of total incapacitation, a new generation of experimenters throughout the nation are showing positive results from rehabilitation, generally with much stronger research bona fides than the research reported in the infamous studies from the "nothing works" era. Tied to time credits for good-behavior, which get prisoners out faster, successful rehabilitative programs could drive down the prison population quickly and keep it down.[28]

None of these ideas is new. They constitute a consensus position even in the relatively law-and-order-oriented expert community. Indeed, California's lead expert at trial was reduced to offering the argument that letting prisoners out early would harm public safety because they would miss out on rehabilitative programs that didn't exist.

At the end of the opinion, the court ordered California to reduce its population by approximately forty thousand prisoners, or find some other way to achieve 137 percent of design capacity, within two years. With a delay for appeals, the state would have even more time. The court let the state choose which, if any, of its recommendations to adopt in achieving this goal, knowing that the state would have to use some major pieces of the court's plan; there was simply no other way to get to the target number.

Because most of the court's proposals point toward diversion of one sort or another rather than criminalizing fewer people to begin with, the population reduction actually will be a transfer from state prisons to probation and perhaps county jails. In short, it is probable that the population of people under correctional custody will remain steady while the state-prison population shrinks. Deeper reforms await political decisions beyond the powers of the court to order. But a benefit of the court-inspired correctional transfer will be an opportunity for innovative approaches to be tested, the most visible and most closely studied penal experiment in recent history.[29] The largely misread and misremembered "nothing works" research about rehabilitative penal practices in the 1970s became part of the common sense supporting incapacitative mass incarceration. There is now hope that better research arising from the population-reduction decision in *Coleman-Plata* can illuminate a better future for prisons, prisoners, and crime prevention.

*   *   *

Once seen by federal courts as a humane solution to the unacceptable crime rates of the 1970s and 1980s, mass incarceration prisons in 2009 were places of extreme peril and suffering. The prisoners they held were imagined as superpredators, convict-revolutionaries, and serial killers, violent deviants whose dangerousness could not be changed. The prisoners of chronic hyper-overcrowding revealed in *Coleman-Plata* belong to a different realm of political imagination, one occupied by pitiful masses—refugees fleeing a war, victims of a natural disaster, populations marked for exclusion, transfer, or elimination. A humanitarian crisis, now so familiar on the world stage, is unexpected and unsettling when identified within the legal system of a wealthy democratic society.

Perhaps nothing epitomizes the plight of the prisoner as "humanitarian subject"—a person vulnerable to all the suffering of the human condition—than the state's use of "dry cells," standing-room-only cages in which seriously mentally ill and suicidal prisoners are held pending transfer to a suicide-watch cell. Dry cells were intended to be used for only a few hours, but stays became much longer because of overcrowding.[30]

The court found that suicidal inmates assigned to mental health crisis beds spent "from Thursday evening to . . . Monday morning" being transferred between dry cells, "tiny, freestanding upright cages with mesh wiring surrounding them (and no toilet)," during the day and wet cells, holding cells with toilets, at night. In several instances, inmates assigned to mental health crisis beds have committed suicide while awaiting transfer.[31] These prisoners were supposed to be transferred to a wet cell at night so they could be monitored to prevent suicide. However, the court noted, "A psychiatric expert reported observing an inmate who had been held in such a cage for nearly 24 hours, standing in a pool of his own urine, unresponsive and nearly catatonic. Prison officials explained they had " 'no place to put him.' "

These images of prisoners undergoing de facto torture, many already chronically ill, massed in spaces of neglect, have begun to replace the forty-year-old images of convict-revolutionaries and serial killers. As this case and the Supreme Court decision that came in its wake show, the federal judiciary is already seeing prisons in a new light. Given the importance that judicial deference has had in making mass incarceration possible and sustainable, that is already an important change. Some four years out from the *Coleman-Plata* decision, it is also clear that these images of suffering and abandonment now compete with the old myths in the public understanding of prisons. The politics of crime fear that produced mass incarceration relied on the image of the prisoner as an unchanging lethal threat. Once the public imagines prisons that hold both high-risk criminals and humanitarian subjects deserving our sympathy, a much more complex and more promising political strategy becomes possible, one in which the state will have to answer hard questions about how its policies sort and distribute risk. The need for a more intelligent, nuanced approach is all the greater because aging convicts at risk of disease and suffering are certain to be a growing portion of the prison population barring dramatic changes in our sentencing laws.

In the conclusion to its 184-page opinion, the court implicitly acknowledged the radical turn it was making, observing that the political nature of mass incarceration justified the court's intervention, just as courts had been required to intervene deeply in school administration to uproot Jim Crow segregation in the South.

> Unfortunately, during the 8 years of the Plata litigation and the 19 years of the Coleman litigation, the political branches of California government charged with addressing the crisis in the state's prisons have failed to do so. Instead, the rights of California's prisoners have repeatedly been ignored. Where the political process has utterly failed to protect the constitutional rights of a minority, the courts can, and must, vindicate those rights.[32]

Demonstrating exactly the reactive commitment to imprisonment that the *Plata-Coleman* court had bemoaned, California appealed the decision, knowing that this would at the very least delay activation of the court's two-year deadline to achieve the population reduction. In doing so, the state relied on two arguments. First, the lawyers argued that under control of the courts, the state was already making sufficient progress toward remedying its unconstitutional conditions. Second, they argued that even though progress toward compliance was slow and inconsistent, the alternative would be to transfer risk from inmates back to the communities that would be endangered by releasing *any* prisoners.

In appealing the ruling of the court, the state was going up against the strong deference that appellate courts owe toward the fact-finding function of trial courts. For California politicians, there was little risk in delaying the reckoning a bit longer. Term limits on legislators and governors induce them to pursue nothing but the shortest-term advantage. Ironically, in pursuing the expedient strategy at the state level, California was making this California-based case into a matter of constitutional principle, turning its own lengthy set of trials into an occasion to put mass incarceration on trial nationally.

6

Dignity Cascade

Brown v. Plata *and Mass Incarceration* *as a Human Rights Problem*

The special three-judge court's population-reduction order, issued in August 2009, required California to bring its swollen prison population down to 137 percent of the capacity of its thirty-three prisons within two years by any means the state chose. The population-reduction order, the largest in history, was justified in an opinion that blamed the continued unconstitutional medical and mental health care delivery in California prisons on the state's sentencing and parole policies, which indiscriminately imprisoned felons regardless of the risk they posed or even the seriousness of their offense. Nearly two years later, in May 2011, the United States Supreme Court upheld both the order and the opinion in its decision in *Brown v. Plata*, named for Governor Jerry Brown, who had succeeded Governor Schwarzenegger in January 2011.[1]

"Prisoners," wrote Justice Anthony Kennedy for a 5–4 majority, "retain the essence of human dignity.... A prison that deprives prisoners of basic sustenance, including adequate medical care, is incompatible with the concept of human dignity and has no place in civilized society."[2] In upholding a systemwide population-reduction order, as opposed to relief for particular prisoners with recognized illnesses, the *Brown* majority made clear that it understood that the problem in California went beyond what individual prisoners had suffered or were likely to suffer and required a remedy designed to force changes deep within the state's mass-incarceration laws and policies. In a footnote (in the law, a way of saying, "Notice this"), Justice Kennedy wrote, "Plaintiffs do not base their case on deficiencies in care provided on any one occasion" but instead

> rely on system-wide deficiencies in the provision of medical and mental health care that, taken as a whole, subject sick and mentally ill prisoners in California to "substantial risk of serious harm" and cause the delivery of care in the prisons to fall below the evolving standards of decency that mark the progress of a maturing society.[3]

Thus *Brown* goes well beyond the landmark 1976 decision *Estelle v. Gamble*, in which the Supreme Court held that depriving a prisoner of necessary medical care violated the Eighth Amendment.

If California's decades-long period of chronic hyper-overcrowding were the exception in America, if the illness burden on its prisoners were unusual, *Brown* might be seen as a remarkable but unique judicial intervention—the *Bush v. Gore* of prison jurisprudence. But *Brown* was not an exception. Overcrowding is the rule in American prisons, and at least a quarter of state prisoners suffer one or more chronic illnesses. Prisoners in most states are subject to the overcrowding and torture that the Court found unconstitutional in *Brown v. Plata*. After the *Brown* appeal, states may choose to incarcerate large segments of their population, but they cannot legally do so on the terms that shaped mass incarceration over the past forty years and took such an extreme form in California.

The consequences of *Brown* in California have been dramatic. The state's prison population has dropped from 156,000 during the trial in 2009 to around 120,000 today.[4] More important, a package of legislation adopted in 2011 expressly to comply with *Brown* has eliminated state prison as a sentencing option for the vast majority of nonviolent, nonserious, nonsexual felonies. The new law shifts responsibility and new funding to counties. Californians convicted of these felonies today may be sentenced at the discretion of county judges to a range of options, including probation. Prisoners released on parole will no longer be supervised by state parole officers, as was the case for more than seventy years. Instead, county probation officers will supervise them, and if they violate the terms of their parole, their sanctions will be determined at the county level. Jail remains an option, but with state prison no longer mandated by rigid laws and policies, mass incarceration in California, for now at least, is dead.

Brown v. Plata has also begun to change the national picture, albeit in more subtle ways. California was not among the first states to move away from indiscriminate use of state prison terms for felonies. That trend began as early as the beginning of the twenty-first century in some states, including Michigan and New York. But with the 2011 population cap imposed by the *Brown* verdict, California has instantly become the leading example of the shift away from state prison. In numbers alone, California is now driving a more robust decline in the imprisonment rate throughout the country than has been seen in decades. Less tangibly, cultural opinion is turning against mass incarceration noticeably faster since the Supreme Court described the country's largest prison system as incompatible with human dignity and the evolving sense of decency in a civilized society.

* * *

Brown v. Plata's most significant and enduring jurisprudential strength may be the opinion's strong affirmation of dignity as a constitutional value with particular relevance to prisons. The majority opinion said:

> As a consequence of their own actions, prisoners may be deprived of rights that are fundamental to liberty. Yet the law and the Constitution demand recognition of certain other rights. Prisoners retain the essence of human dignity inherent in all persons. Respect for that dignity animates the Eighth Amendment prohibition against cruel and unusual punishment. "The basic concept underlying the Eighth Amendment is nothing less than the dignity of man."[5]

The word *dignity* appears nowhere in the U.S. Constitution, but it has been used more than nine hundred times by the Supreme Court in its opinions.[6] Still, compared to concepts such as liberty and equality, dignity has played a marginal role until now, especially with respect to individual rights.[7] The Supreme Court has historically referred to dignity in terms of three distinct issues: the dignity of states (and sometimes Indian tribes), the dignity of courts, and human dignity. Only the last bears on prisons and punishment. For much of the nineteenth century, dignity was reserved for the states and the federal government, on which the honors and dignities of monarchy had descended.

Human dignity had been acknowledged as an important value underlying the Eighth Amendment's ban on cruel and unusual punishment.[8] But in the decades before the *Brown v. Plata* decision, it had fallen into a kind of oblivion and was not seen as a basis for running or evaluating prisons. *Brown v. Plata* is a potential turning point toward a future when American political leaders and prison planners are forced to justify the effect of imprisonment on both public safety *and prisoners*. While the vote in *Brown* was close (5–4), the split on the Supreme Court now favors a constitutional commitment to human dignity over the court's decades-long deference to states' policies and prison administrators.[9]

Brown v. Plata is the most recent instance of a "dignity cascade." I offer this term to describe moments when a society recognizes that it has profoundly violated human dignity and in response expands its very understanding of what humanity includes and requires of the law. A dignity cascade can lead long-rigid legal meanings to become fluid and long-tolerated practices to be recognized as unlawful. A global dignity cascade began in 1948 when recognition of Nazi war crimes led the victorious nations to sign the Universal Declaration of Human Rights, the foundational document for modern international human rights standards. An even earlier example was the reaction to jail fever (typhus epidemics in prisons), which gave rise to the legal concept of the prisoner as a human being and helped shape the design of penitentiaries to acknowledge the humanity of inmates. In the nineteenth century, a similar anxiety about the treatment of wounded and captured soldiers in European wars led to the formation of the International Committee of the Red Cross and the Geneva Convention of 1864.[10]

* * *

The Supreme Court gave its first modern nod to dignity as a human right in the 1958 case of *Trop v. Dulles* at the height of the Cold War and a decade after the Universal Declaration of Human Rights. In this unusual Supreme Court decision finding a specific noncapital sentence unconstitutional, the Court held Trop's punishment—loss of his U.S. citizenship as a punishment for desertion from the military—cruel and unusual. Chief Justice Warren, writing for a plurality of four justices, asserted, "The basic concept underlying the Eighth Amendment is nothing less than the dignity of man."[11] Unfortunately, this was the closest a dignity view of the Eighth Amendment came to receiving majority support.

Fourteen years later, in *Furman v. Georgia* (1972), in which a divided majority struck down the death penalty as then carried out in the United States, Justice Brennan wrote a concurring opinion that extended and refined the dignity view of the Eighth Amendment. His eloquent disquisition on dignity, perhaps intended for a majority that never coalesced, may represent the most developed account in our constitutional tradition of the meaning of dignity for punishment until now. It is worth quoting at length:

> At bottom, then, the Cruel and Unusual Punishments Clause prohibits the infliction of uncivilized and inhuman punishments. The State, even as it punishes, must treat its members with respect for their intrinsic worth as human beings. A punishment is "cruel and unusual," therefore, if it does not comport with human dignity. . . .
>
> More than the presence of pain, however, is comprehended in the judgment that the extreme severity of a punishment makes it degrading to the dignity of human beings. The barbaric punishments condemned by history, "punishments which inflict torture, such as the rack, the thumbscrew, the iron boot, the stretching of limbs and the like," are, of course, "attended with acute pain and suffering." . . . When we consider why they have been condemned, however, we realize that the pain involved is not the only reason. The true significance of these punishments is that they treat members of the human race as nonhumans, as objects to be toyed with and discarded. They are thus inconsistent with the fundamental premise of the Clause that even the vilest criminal remains a human being possessed of common human dignity.[12]

Although addressing capital punishment, Brennan's opinion emphasizes dehumanization; his insistence that the clear rejection of torture in the history of the Eighth Amendment is part of a larger commitment to human dignity that forbids treating "members of the human race as nonhumans, as objects to be toyed with and discarded," carried considerable implications for the coming storm of criminal justice practices, including supermax prisons, lengthy drug-crime sentences aimed at deterring others, and recidivist laws demanding incapacitation without end. If Justice Brennan's opinion had been for a majority (instead of being one of several concurring opinions in a divided majority), not only would capital punishment have ended in the United States in 1972; it is also very likely that mass incarceration would never have happened. As it was, Brennan's opinion was a glimpse of what a dignity-based jurisprudence of the Eighth Amendment might have looked like. Four years later, in 1976, when a majority of justices voted to uphold a number of new capital-sentencing schemes, Justice Brennan's opinion was a dissent, and that's where dignity as a restraining value on punishment remained for the rest of the twentieth century.

During the buildup of mass incarceration in the 1980s and 1990s, the Supreme Court altogether ceased talking about dignity in relation to imprisonment. Instead, that period's most significant decision on the meaning of "cruel and unusual punishment," based on facts that epitomized the extreme sentencing policies of that era, was Justice Kennedy's opinion in *Harmelin v. Michigan*, which held that the Eighth Amendment imposed practically *no* limits on punishment. Kennedy developed a set of principles that emphasized the freedom of the state to choose its criminal justice objectives and then pursue them subject only to the scarcest degree of rational credibility.

The *Harmelin* case challenged a mandatory sentence of life without parole for possession of more than 656 grams (1.45 pounds) of crack cocaine, arguing that the sentence was so disproportionate as to constitute cruel and unusual punishment. A majority rejected the view, beginning a line of such victories for extreme penalties. Justice Kennedy, in what would prove an influential concurrence, spelled out no fewer than five principles that should lead courts to exercise extreme deference in reviewing prison sentences. Kennedy wrote:

> All of these principles—the primacy of the legislature, the variety of legitimate penological schemes, the nature of our federal system, and the requirement that proportionality review be guided by objective factors—inform the final one: The Eighth Amendment does not require strict proportionality between crime and sentence. Rather, it forbids only extreme sentences that are "grossly disproportionate" to the crime.[13]

During the same decades, European states pursued a very different path. Thanks to the European Convention on Human Rights, dignity has become a central value regulating the nature and limits of imprisonment.[14] Article 3 states that "No one shall be subjected to torture or to inhuman or degrading treatment or punishment." The same language is used in Article 5 of the Universal Declaration of Human Rights. Far from being limited to a right against torture, in Europe, the idea that prisoners must have their humanity respected even as they are being punished has produced rights within prison regimes that promote individualization, normalization, and the preparation of all prisoners for the possibility of return to the community.[15] These principles bind the prison systems in the member states of the Council of Europe to the goal of minimizing imprisonment.[16]

The reach of human rights norms as a counterweight to punitive populism in Europe owes much to the development of specialized governmental organs that support this mission, especially the Committee for the Prevention of Torture and the Council of Europe's Committee of Ministers. These organizations include representatives from all the member states in the

European community and have specialized expertise and authority. They have produced a body of norms ("soft law"—authoritative but not binding rules) governing the treatment of prisoners. These norms extend well beyond the specific prohibitions of the European Court of Human Rights. They have in fact encouraged the expansion of those binding protections.

The Committee for the Prevention of Torture is authorized to inspect prisons and other places of detention throughout the member states without prior notice or approval. In practice, the committee generally provides notice, however. Their inspections and the reports they produce (officially, private reports to the member government, but in almost every case published with the approval of the government) are designed to prevent degrading or inhumane punishment or treatment from developing and thus do not focus on whether current practices constitute a violation of the European Convention. Member governments are not obliged to correct the problems identified, or even respond, but they generally do, and human rights concepts, such as prohibition of degrading treatment, have been influential on the European Court's interpretation of Article 3.[17]

The Committee of Ministers is the quasi-legislative branch of the European Community. Its members, typically high ministers in the member governments, produce reports and norms on all issues bearing on convention-protected rights. Since the 1990s, the committee has produced a comprehensive set of norms for the protection of convention rights in prisons, the European Prison Rules (last updated in 2006). These rules are authoritative for all member states, and while prisoners may not be successful in seeking legal redress for violations, the rules have been regularly cited by the European Court of Human Rights. Moreover, because ministers of the member state governments have been directly involved in developing the rules, there is a strong presumption that the rules should be treated as objectives by all of the prison services.

Although U.S. federal courts have far greater power than even the European Court of Human Rights to compel an end to conditions that violate the Constitution, U.S. law lacks human rights norms and institutions to counterbalance the kind of populist hysteria that led to total incapacitation. Without institutions like the Committee for the Prevention of Torture and the Committee of Ministers, even as dignity gains wider recognition as a constitutional value, its reach into the administration of prisons will still depend on case-by-case litigation before individual federal judges all over the country and thus be more episodic and less comprehensive.[18]

Brown v. Plata could encourage more vigilance by those federal judges by bringing dignity back into Eighth Amendment law, where it can literally "animate" the arid terms of the ban on "cruel and unusual punishment."[19] That language originated in the English Bill of Rights in 1689, a time when state punishment consisted mostly of public floggings, humiliation, and executions. The words provide very little help in setting limits to punishments that rely primarily on incarceration. *Brown* reminds us that prison conditions can amount to torture: not just singular acts of extreme medical and mental health suffering, of which the Court documented many, but also the constant exposure of thousands of prisoners to the real risk of what Justice Kennedy described as "prolonged illness and unnecessary pain"[20] if their chronic conditions remain untreated or if they need prompt treatment for a serious condition.[21] It is this routine, incremental torture in mass incarceration prisons that *Brown* brings into the ambit of the Eighth Amendment ban. Thus *Brown* has the potential to call many aspects of prisons and penal policy into question.

As expected, Justice Antonin Scalia, writing for himself and Justice Thomas in dissent, assailed the idea that a systemwide deficiency could constitute an Eighth Amendment violation, let alone torture:

The plaintiffs do not appear to claim—and it would be absurd to suggest—that every single one of those prisoners has personally experienced "torture or a lingering death" . . . as a consequence of that bad medical system. Indeed, it is inconceivable that anything more than a small proportion of prisoners in the plaintiff classes have personally received sufficiently atrocious treatment that their Eighth Amendment right was violated.[22]

Justice Scalia recognized that the *Brown* majority represents a significant widening of the protection previously thought offered by the Eighth Amendment in the area of medical care, from extreme moments of deprivation to a systemic denial of adequate care. This has extraordinary implications at a time when chronic illness, which requires consistent treatment and individualized caregiving, is becoming the dominant health problem facing prisons and society. Once we recognize that chronic illnesses incrementally exact irreparable harm when they are neglected, sentencing a disease-burdened population to mass incarceration–style imprisonment places them at a constitutionally unacceptable risk of torture should their disease follow its natural course. For Justice Scalia, though, the Eighth Amendment protects only those prisoners actually experiencing torture at any given moment, and only a remedy limited to them would be sufficiently narrow to meet the requirements of the Prison Litigation Reform Act.[23] Torture under Scalia's definition would rarely if ever be litigated while it is occurring, leaving prisoners protected only against the most intentional assaults on their bodies.

The broader understanding of torture and the enhanced vision of dignity in *Brown* stands in stark contrast to a series of decisions in the 1980s and 1990s in which the court pronounced a doctrine of increasing deference to state prisons and their administrative judgments.[24] Although framed in Eighth Amendment platitudes, these decisions were anchored in historically limited assumptions about the overall severity of crime and the generalized dangerousness of anyone who breaks any one of an ever-broadening list of felonies, assumptions which have little contemporary relevance and deserve little respect in future court decisions. While we normally view judicial restraint as making room for democratic decision making, in the era of mass incarceration, the extreme deference led to political paralysis. Unquestioned state "preferences" in criminal justice objectives and administrators' "discretion" over prison operations grew into a punitive power limited by no democratic or professional restraints, unable to modulate itself to achieve social gains. California became the poster child for this pathology, but most states have powerful advocates of extreme punishment in their legislatures and prison bureaucracies, who push the system toward more incarceration and will be formidable obstacles to reform.

The question left to us by *Brown v. Plata* is whether the enhanced status of dignity as an Eighth Amendment value, along with court challenges to a host of mass-incarceration practices, can break up those dense blocks of punitive power, compelling legislators and administrators to revisit and rebalance a system that clearly overimprisons people with little relationship to an individual's moral blameworthiness or a realistic assessment of his future dangerousness.

The past suggests that the Supreme Court, though it opened the door, is not likely to be the most active or important player. In our legal system, cases are based on the factual record developed in litigation before a trial court. Judges are bound to the specific circumstances exposed by the advocates, and the application of their rulings to subsequent cases with even slightly different facts is always contestable and frequently limited. California's extreme overcrowding and its equally extreme commitment to total incapacitation may limit the application of *Brown* to the more restrained versions of mass incarceration operating in many states.[25]

However, it is also possible that the Supreme Court's response to the abominable facts will shake up the punishment establishment.[26] *Brown* may signal a shift in viewing prison-condition claims from a civil rights framework to a human rights framework. The civil rights framework, borrowed by prisoner advocates from the legal battle against racial segregation during the middle of the twentieth century, gained traction from the 1940s through the 1970s and achieved what many considered a revolution in the legal status and material conditions of state prisoners in that era. However, that progress depended on conditions that were soon to change dramatically, especially on the superficial national commitment to rehabilitation, which soon collapsed.[27]

The civil rights framework has proven far less effective in preventing or contesting mass incarceration, for several reasons. Without a commitment to rehabilitation, neither equality claims nor liberty claims (based on failures of due process) have much traction. If a prison system is formally committed to rehabilitation, for example by linking parole release to evidence of personal reform, a prisoner might claim that he has been denied equal access to rehabilitative programs based on race or that his liberty (parole) is being arbitrarily denied. But if incapacitation is the official goal, these claims melt away, because prisoners already have equal opportunities for boredom and misery, and the system, which now makes no promises, can't be penalized for breaking any.

If *Brown v. Plata* does begin a new wave of legal intervention in the U.S. prisons, it won't be because it introduces a new doctrine; for the most part, it restates and reaffirms existing constitutional precedents. It will be because it offers a new perspective on prisons and prisoners. The silencing of federal judicial criticism of American prisons beginning in the 1970s stemmed from the new "realism" about prisons, prisoners, and crime prevention that reduced prisoner civil rights to cramped applications of existing precedents.[28]

Brown represents a different way of seeing prisons and prisoners. This becomes most evident in the vivid and disturbing images of prisoners and suffering that are presented, culminating in the remarkable photographs of California prison conditions appended to the majority opinion. Pictures and other images of beings in pain intensify the intrinsic human ability to empathize, to connect to emotions of sympathy and outrage. That's why literature, and later photography and videography, have been essential to the spread of the global human rights movement.

The image of the so-called dry cages that the justices appended to their decision in the *Brown* case is perhaps the most powerful in the entire corpus of evidence presented. The record describes their function as providing suicide prevention for mentally ill prisoners awaiting transfer to secure treatment beds for what the Supreme Court described as a "prolonged period." The cages in the photo are empty. We may imagine but do not see prisoners suffering from psychotic delusions

Salinas Valley State Prison, July 29, 2008. Correctional Treatment Center: dry cages, holding cells for people waiting for mental health treatment.

and powerful impulses of self-destruction. Left to stand na-ked, with no place to lie down or to relieve themselves, these absent prisoners embody degradation. The cages, standing in a line that extends beyond the frame of the photograph (inviting us to imagine a line that just keeps going), evoke the high con-centration of mentally ill prisoners and California's failure, de-spite two decades of litigation and two major reform orders, to see prisoners as human beings and to give them even the most basic care required for their fundamental dignity.

If the dry cage evokes the loss of human individuality and dignity by its emptiness, two other images also attached to the opinion reveal the loss of these qualities within the multitudes of the desperate. These photos show rows of "bad beds," Cali-fornia's own bureaucratic name for bunk beds crammed cha-otically into areas of California prisons designed for work, treatment, and medical care, where thousands of California prisoners have spent most of their time.

These two photos show scenes of chaotic crowding and prisoners milling about with few guards and little to keep the inmates occupied except scattered television sets mounted high on the wall. The two photos, taken two years apart at two different prisons, helped confirm the basic finding that chronic hyper-overcrowding had overwhelmed the ability of managers to reform prison health care or maintain basic human dignity. The time lapse speaks to political leaders' lack of commitment to obey previous court orders.

The top one, from the California Institution for Men in 2006, is taken from the ground and gives us a perspective like that of prisoners as they walk along the corridor between rows of stacked bunks, which became a major artery of movement within the prison. We can imagine being vulnerable to assault from someone in the crowd who has had enough and suddenly lashes out, all the more so if either the victim or the perpetrator or both are mentally ill. The prisoner in a wheelchair is a

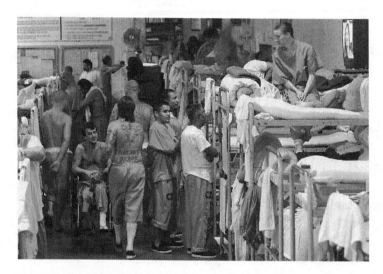

California Institution for Men, August 7, 2006.

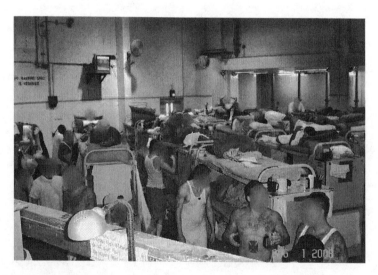

Mule Creek State Prison, August 1, 2008.

prominent reminder of the ubiquity of disability and chronic illness there. He makes his way along the same corridor using a foot and his hands to propel himself forward while other prisoners flow around him.

The second photograph, taken two years later at Mule Creek State Prison, shows a view from above the main floor of an irregular housing unit. From this perspective of authority, as it were, we see the sheer density of human bodies in vertical space, stacked in the bunks and standing in the corridors between them. In an attack or medical emergency, a person would be in the hands of fellow prisoners for a long time before prison officers could get there.

These photos give the lie to claims of the legitimacy of mass incarceration, that prisons are a secure and humane way to deal with unacceptable threats to the community's safety. These images usher us not into that fantasy prison but into a refugee camp. They show the sort of humanitarian crisis that we're so used to seeing on the news, about lands far away.[29]

The suffering of people caught up in humanitarian crises does something remarkable and does it reliably: it evokes empathy, a feeling of "There but for the grace of God go I." Since the Enlightenment, a whole new kind of humanitarian reasoning has arisen that makes the visible suffering of people the focus and rationale for political arguments and legal institutions.[30] Alongside this reasoning has developed a new sector of governing power anchored in international networks of expertise and activism rather than sovereignty—what we now call nongovernmental organizations (NGOs).

Feelings of empathy interrupted oral argument over the *Brown v. Plata* appeal in December 2010. Justice Breyer tersely ordered California's lawyer to look at the photo of dry cages in an amicus brief filed by a group of religious organizations. His voice was edged with anger as he rhetorically asked, "Now, you've looked at them. I've looked at them. And what is the answer to that? So how can I—or you if you were in my position—what would you say?"[31]

Justice Breyer expressed anger mixed with disgust, or fear, but also with a sense of personal responsibility. This response, which might be called humanitarian anxiety, plays a critical role in dignity cascades. During these moments, images of suffering among those previously beneath the notice of powerful legal elites (politicians, judges, lawyers) generate a sense of revulsion at current practices and a motivation to reform them in the name of decency. When a dignity cascade ensues, the circuit between image, revulsion, anxiety, and moral resolve is self-sustaining for a time, leading to dramatic change in the legal status of those previously dehumanized.

Images of disease in prison have been a powerful driver of reform since the late eighteenth century.[32] The body in pain, disease, and abandonment calls forth empathy, bridging the gulf that prison opens between the punished and the free, a gulf that was far more permeable before the birth of the penitentiary.[33]

So far, the suffering portrayed in *Brown v. Plata* has caused humanitarian anxiety only among judges, but they are probably the most important audience it could reach. In America, the judiciary is the institution most accessible to the excluded and outcast, particularly prisoners. The federal judiciary has long been chastened by a fear that judicial interventions helped make prisons more dangerous by enforcing civil rights orders that limited the discretion of administrators. The resulting extreme deference now seems to be ending. The images appended by Justice Kennedy to his majority opinion in *Brown* are there because they reflect what brought Justice Kennedy into the majority, and they are helping to create a new understanding of the prison situation among judges and perhaps more broadly. Moreover, because the pictures come packaged with legal doctrine relevant to future cases, the humanitarian anxiety experienced by the Supreme Court majority in examining the record in *Brown* ("supreme humanitarian anxiety"?) invites more litigation about prison conditions and inhumane aspects of mass incarceration, which in turn has the potential to generate more images and more humanitarian anxiety. This is how a dignity cascade can continue to gather momentum.

Of course, we should have no illusions that a dignity cascade about prisons alone will overcome the concentration of the negative effects of criminalization and mass incarceration on communities of color. The history of dignity suggests that reforms aimed at protecting an enhanced understanding of human rights often fail to achieve equality; these reforms regularly fall short for those already low in social status by virtue of their race or color, gender, class, and/or queerness.[34] But this awareness must inform our effort to interpret and implement dignity rather than discourage us from claiming human rights for the victims of mass incarceration.

* * *

If *Brown v. Plata* had been focused solely on the suffering of prisoners, the case might have been destined to join a noble pantheon of cases in which the court has defended "evolving standards of decency" without changing much of anything. However, because in *Brown* the justices were compelled by the Prison Litigation Reform Act explicitly to address public safety issues in determining whether a population cap was necessary, they had to go further and question the premise that prisons reduce the threat of violence to the community.

Writing for the majority in *Brown v. Plata*, Justice Kennedy acknowledged the risks of "premature release" of prisoners:

High recidivism rates must serve as a warning that mistaken or premature release of even one prisoner can cause injury and harm. The release of prisoners in large numbers—assuming the State finds no other way to comply with the order—is a matter of undoubted, grave concern.[35]

Justice Scalia in his dissent put the matter as starkly as possible.

There comes before us, now and then, a case whose proper outcome is so clearly indicated by tradition and *common sense*, that its decision ought to shape the law, rather than vice versa. One would think that, before allowing the decree of a federal district court to release 46,000 convicted felons, this Court would bend every effort to read the law in such a way as to avoid that outrageous result. Today, quite to the contrary, the Court disregards stringently drawn provisions of the governing statute, and traditional constitutional limitations upon the power of a federal judge, in order to uphold the absurd.[36]

Justice Alito was even more alarmist. Noting at the outset of his dissent that the 46,000 prisoners who would be released amounted to some two army divisions of criminals presumably assaulting innocent Californians, he ended his dissent with perhaps the grimmest concluding sentences in Supreme Court history.

I fear that today's decision, like prior prisoner release orders, will lead to a grim roster of victims. I hope that I am wrong. In a few years, we will see.[37]

In quietly affirming the lower court's evidence-based assessment that prison was not a necessary or sufficient condition of public safety, the *Brown* majority broke with the posture of extreme deference toward imprisonment choices and unleashed a potential sea change in penal policy. For decades the consolidation of all branches of state and local governments behind incapacitation has helped make imprisonment America's default mode of punishing even those crimes where there is no victim, let alone a strong victim lobby for harsh penalties. It was a form of "common sense," as Justice Scalia put it, that was safely beyond empirical assessment but could be used as a litmus test to determine whether a decision-maker supported ordinary citizens or dangerous deviants. This reflexive preference for imprisonment became the impetus for total incapacitation that pushed California's prisons into the abyss. Justice Kennedy, drawing on the extensive expert testimony produced by the three-judge court's fourteen-day trial, questioned this illogical logic with empirical evidence and expert assessment:

> Expert witnesses produced statistical evidence that prison populations had been lowered without adversely affecting public safety in a number of jurisdictions, including certain counties in California, as well as Wisconsin, Illinois, Texas, Colorado, Montana, Michigan, Florida, and Canada. . . . Washington's former secretary of corrections testified that his State had implemented population reduction methods, including parole reform and expansion of good time credits, without any "deleterious effect on crime." . . . In light of this evidence, the three-judge court concluded that any negative impact on public safety would be "substantially offset, and perhaps entirely eliminated, by the public safety benefits" of a reduction in overcrowding.[38]

Thus by forcing the court to consider explicitly the threat to public safety of releasing large numbers of prisoners, the Prison Litigation Reform Act had an unintended consequence: the Supreme Court found the threat to be minimal. This finding in turn has huge implications for the future of incarceration based on fear and practiced at a mass scale.

* * *

Brown's immediate mandate is to California, whose road to a constitutional prison system will be long. But the majority's clarion call that "dignity animates the Eighth amendment" is a warning shot to any state engaging in mass imprisonment. The decision's reach will also be long. In scale—size of class, breadth of the order, size of the prisoner population reduction ordered, and degree of interference with state law—*Brown* is a magnitude larger than any prisoner-rights case in a generation. It reverses an almost unbroken movement by both the Supreme Court and Congress to affirm the sanctity of state judgments about prison and deference to the expertise of prison administrators.

In reviving decades-old language about dignity and civilized behavior, the majority seemed to draw a broad lesson from the extraordinary deprivations tolerated by California (and by the court itself in the past). Prison conditions such as those in California's "security housing units," which were largely upheld against Eighth Amendment challenge in *Madrid v. Gomez*[39] at the beginning of this round of litigation in the mid-1990s, must be reconsidered under *Brown's* enhanced vision of the role of dignity in interpreting the Eighth Amendment. Life without parole, long terms on death row followed by execution, stigmatizing and degrading treatment of arrestees, and the endless collateral legal disabilities that tend to keep ex-cons unemployed without public assistance, all but forcing them back into crime—all these and many other seemingly unassailable state penal policies are now open to challenge.

These arguments will begin in courts. But if they are to transform the culture of fear that has blighted American democracy, they must spread to the broader public. *Brown v. Plata* offers an opportunity to forge a new common sense about prisons, prisoners, and crime.

7

The New Common Sense
of High-Crime Societies

Every Supreme Court case changes the law. Some cases have the potential to change society.

Technically, the three-judge court and the Supreme Court left California free to build new prisons or outsource its prisoners to Mexico, but the only practical way to achieve the reduction was to reform state law to prevent the routine use of state imprisonment in managing its felon population. Thus the decision came very close to mandating the end of mass incarceration in California as a matter of law and administration.

Brown v. Plata put the human dignity of prisoners back at the constitutional center of the Eighth Amendment. Reaffirming language used more tentatively in the past (in concurrences by Chief Justice Earl Warren and Associate Justice William Brennan),[1] the *Brown* majority condemned as "uncivilized" California's prolonged tolerance of inhumane conditions. But this state-specific and clearly well-deserved judicial shaming was coupled with the majority's general warning to other states: "Respect for that [human] dignity animates the

Eighth Amendment prohibition against cruel and unusual punishment."

In the short term, *Brown* has already encouraged a wave of new prisoner claims that seemed unlikely only a short time ago. Dignity-infused arguments under the Eighth Amendment (and also under the Fourth, Fifth, and Sixth Amendments, as well as under the broad due-process promises of the Fifth and Fourteenth) appear promising in the effort to undercut the outdated presumptions that had sustained mass incarceration in the courts. Each lawsuit will offer another political opportunity to challenge the assumptions that inform our so-called high-crime and definitely high-incarceration society.[2]

The 2011 *Brown v. Plata* decision is timely; it arrived at a moment when the window for policy change in criminal justice is more open than it has been in decades.[3] The case will have its greatest impact if it helps form the new common sense about prisons, prisoners, and crime prevention that is emerging today in the United States. This new common sense derives from many sources, starting with the significant drop in violent crime over the past two decades. Optimism about crime-prevention strategies is also contributing, along with better approaches to handling the mental illnesses that can lead to prison.

The old common sense of our "high-crime society" was born in the 1970s "years of fear" that led to consensus of sorts behind mass incarceration. This consensus was never homogeneous or uncontested. It was an emotional attitude that crystallized in the intense media and political attention given to a few pivotal events around prisons early in that decade. Of course not everyone shared that view, but everyone who tried to speak or act on prison issues in the intervening decades has had to deal with it.

The old common sense about *prisons* was captured succinctly in the phrase that Anthony Kennedy, then a judge of the Court of Appeals for the Ninth Circuit, wrote some thirty-five years ago in *Spain v. Procunier*—that prisons serve the "unenviable task of keeping dangerous men secure in humane conditions." Restated by the Supreme Court in *Farmer v. Brennan*, that seemingly modest formula has encouraged courts to rely on the expertise and goodwill of prison officials.

These fear-based prisons may not rehabilitate, but they *are* good at keeping order and control, at least if they operate at normal capacity.[4] Above all, the common sense presumed, they are humane. This assumption seemed reasonable in the 1980s when many states, some under court orders, were building new prisons. At the same time, the American correctional profession seemed solidly anchored to the civilized and humane standards of rehabilitation-oriented correctionalism.

The old common sense about *prisoners* was that they were a sample of a permanent criminal *class* whose threat of future felonies was not precisely knowable but presumptively high and unchanging. Prisoners in general were imagined as zombies, superpredators whose threat doesn't change with time or maturation.[5] High levels of violence in American society were assumed to reflect the concentration of superpredators in our midst and the likelihood that their numbers would grow. Superpredators engaged in all kinds of crime—drug, property, and violent—indeed, their very lifestyle seemed to be a kind of crime, "gang behavior." They couldn't be deterred or rehabilitated, so incapacitation was the only solution to crime. If zombies embody our fear of crime in the period of the "superpredator" and mass incarceration, the recent rococo silliness of fantasies about a "zombie apocalypse" suggests that this mythology may finally be dying out—that our sense of irony is now too keen for the fears of the 1970s and 1980s.

The old common sense about *crime prevention*, laid down in the 1970s, relied almost exclusively on incapacitating dedicated offenders whose individual recidivism had become alarmingly high and resistant to alternative sentencing and rehabilitative programs. The best empirical research of the 1970s, sponsored by federal agencies hoping to reassure the public about crime, found little support for the idea that more effective deployment of more police could help. Police were believed to be able to do little more than arrest superpredators and collect the evidence necessary for prosecutors to take advantage of the growing stock of enhanced sentencing laws, which mandated longer and longer sentences even for nonviolent crimes and the ever-growing list of victimless pseudocrimes. It no longer mattered much what crime the arrestees had actually committed or whether they had committed any crime at all. All hope for crime relief lay in arresting as many people as possible, making their conviction a foregone conclusion, and giving them long, inflexible prison sentences. States expanded their prisons substantially and enacted laws favoring mass imprisonment and eliminating opportunities for early release.

Because the emotionally charged experiences underlying this late-twentieth-century phenomenon are specific to the generations that lived through them, they are finite, but their influence could last a long time, especially because larger percentages of the elderly vote than do the young. Baby Boomers, who came of age during the fear years, are particularly crucial to engage in reworking our common sense about prisons, prisoners, and crime prevention, given their outsize influence and wealth.[6] The content and strength of this new common sense will help determine how quickly we can repair the extraordinary damage that mass incarceration has done to our democracy and society, as well as what kind of criminal justice system emerges to take its place.

Much of the new common sense about criminal justice has been circulating for years in specialist communities, including criminologists, anti-incarceration activists, and some philanthropists and foundation directors. Today it is being taken up by a few media outlets and rising politicians.

Brown v. Plata has revealed that prisons hold many people who are not a danger to anyone, perhaps never were, and could certainly be managed with less danger to themselves and no additional danger to others through alternatives to prison. Many of these prisoners are burdened with multiple chronic illnesses, including mental illness, which is irreversibly worsened by incarceration, even when health care is provided up to the Constitution's minimal standards. Mass imprisonment creates an unsustainable financial burden in responsible states that invest in mental health and medical care to prisoners. In states such as California, however, where prisons were built with deliberate indifference to the needs of prisoners, it will continue to create humanitarian disasters.

In the new common sense, the urge to imprison is counterbalanced by a keen awareness of the terribly high costs of incarceration in long-term consequences for the health of prisoners and the fiscal condition of our health care system. This new common sense embraces a principle of parsimony in the use of prison that was already being adopted by many states after World War II, before fear of the growing crime wave in the 1960s swept away decades of criminological and penal knowledge.[7]

A consensus now exists among criminologists that states should be addressing many nonviolent, nonserious crimes—even many now classed as felonies—with some combination of fines (which can be made income neutral), restorative justice, enhanced probation (including treatment, electronic monitoring, and home arrest when warranted by risk assessment), and very short terms in local jails.

Gradations in punishment offer real ways to calibrate the seriousness with which society takes various level of crimes, as well as ways to deter others. California's own "realignment plan," a package of legislation adopted in 2011 to comply with the *Brown v. Plata* decision, shifts penalties for many of California's nonviolent, nonserious, and nonsexual felons, as well as most parole violators, from prison to options including those mentioned above. The outcome of this realignment is still undetermined, and its ambitions remain understated. However, the plan, which is in its third year as of this writing and likely to expand, is the strongest indicator yet that this new common sense about prisons can take hold at the level of state legislatures.

While reforms aimed at moving low-level violators out of prison are fast becoming a new common sense, the fate of felony offenders whose crime is so serious that prison time is a compelling choice also needs a new vision. A sentence to prison must never be a sentence to be treated in a degrading manner or to have one's human dignity defiled and denied, as has been the case in much of the United States for a generation. Going forward, however, we must do more than merely conserving some minimal level of human dignity. When we sentence someone to prison, those prisons must be places designed to *counter* rather than exacerbate the predictable deterioration in health and mental stability. This also will require a rescaling of sentences, so that the deterrent and retributive value of incarceration can be achieved without the long, atavistic tail of total incapacitation being routinely applied. Sentences over five years should be reserved for only the most serious crimes.[8]

Prison health care, both mental and physical, must be at the very center of a new penal regime for several reasons. The expulsion of medicine from the prisons led custodial conditions to deteriorate rapidly once population pressures built. By contrast, a robust health care screening and delivery system is the only reliable way to counter mass incarceration's effect on prison conditions. Medical care also provides a framework for individualization, which is essential if human dignity is to be preserved against the relentless dehumanization of prison. While this will raise the short-term costs of incarceration (and appropriately price it against nonincarcerative penalties that do not require medical services), it will reduce its long-term costs while preventing the slide toward cruel, inhuman, and degrading treatment.

The new common sense will likely see a move away from megaprisons toward smaller ones specialized for particular ages and sentence conditions. If shorter sentences are adopted, more of these can be served in jails closer to the communities to which prisoners will be returning. Jails can make better use of pretrial release programs to keep their space available for when it is truly needed. Likewise, when very long sentences are applied for crimes such as murder, rape, and kidnapping, the prison regime must be designed to conserve dignity and health through programs that permit individuals to mark progress toward meaningful life objectives, through education, work, or connections to family life on the outside. For all but the most extreme crimes or the oldest serious offenders, such a system must include a realistic hope of returning to the community before the end of life. Such hope is the main line of any dignity-conserving regime and the best mechanism to encourage good behavior in prison. Even in cases where old age or the seriousness of the crime makes a real life after prison unrealistic, nobody should have to die in prison.[9]

The new common sense understands crime as highly situational and often regulated by routine activities. Commission of actual crimes is most likely to be triggered by short-term shifts in opportunities to commit them, not the innate differences in character that our normal accounts of crime point to. Even repeat or violent offenders tend to commit violent crimes only episodically, and even then only at peak periods in their life course, which tend to diminish rapidly with maturation—unless prison or subsequent isolation as a result of prison keeps people from building a dignified life outside of prison.

Criminological research provides a robust picture of crime over the course of life.[10] Criminal acts rise in youth and young adulthood, then diminish rapidly in middle age. Total incapac-itation has no place for such change. Zombies and superpreda-tors don't have life stages; they're already dead, or dead to society. All we can do is destroy them or contain them.

The crisis of chronic illness unfolding in American prisons tells a different story. Prisoners *do* have life stages; their bodies age. They change and often mature. When this happens largely in prison (or in and out of prison), the change is mostly for the worse, especially in terms of health. Chronic illnesses get worse if one is prevented from trying to make them better. Prison makes them much, much worse. For almost all adults, the crime and illness curves run inversely; the risk of crime starts high and ends up low, while the risk of illness starts off low (al-though injury risk may be high in the working years for some) and ends up high.

Prisoners exist in the same universe as everyone else. They may have started off at a higher rate of criminal behavior than the average citizen, and the slope of their criminal-risk decline may be shallower, but the slope is assuredly there; it ends at the same place for everyone—very low crime rates, followed eventually by death.

Many prisoners start off incarceration with a higher risk of bad health than members of the same age group not facing prison, and years of prison accelerate the age-related decline. Prisoners are considered geriatric at fifty-five, ten years earlier than the nonincarcerated. In short, all prisoners have a time during which their risk of committing a serious crime while free diminishes as their risk of suffering a serious health con-sequence from being in prison increases. A prison regime that closes its eyes to these population-wide but individual pro-cesses is likely to achieve very small public-safety gains at the cost of much money and much more inhumanity. California made this trade-off for a generation.

The new common sense about crime prevention is that a great deal can be done to lower crime by regulating the routine activities and situations in which crimes repeatedly occur. Much violent crime in the 1980s, for example, appears to have been a function of outdoor drug markets that attracted robberies and rival gang attacks. Part of the crime decline in the 1990s was due to efforts by police to force drug markets to move off the streets. This did not necessarily prevent drug dealing, but it did eliminate much of the violent crime associated with it. Whatever its precise causes, the crime decline since the 1990s disproves the myth of unchangeable individual criminality, according to which long-term crime declines should be possible only by reducing the number of young adults (those in the more crime-prone years) or by locking more people up. Instead, the decline in violent crime seems mostly to have been achieved by subtler changes in behavior by both police and communities.

A great deal more research needs to be done before anyone should be confident that we know what mix of better police tactics, changing patterns of behavior among youth, or other unobserved changes in the social context are best for reducing crime. However, the current record strongly suggests that mass incarceration is not a necessary ingredient of crime prevention.

The last decade and a half have seen the emergence of a set of assumptions about prisons, prisoners, and crime prevention opposite to those that lined up behind mass incarceration. This has given us the best opening in fifty years to reinvent our approach to public safety. The *Brown v. Plata* three-judge court's recommendations for how to reduce the prison population without producing more crime is a tool kit for this reinvention; it's already being used in California's realignment policy and can be employed elsewhere.

* * *

One important source of a new common sense is the decline in crime that American cities have experienced, undoing the increases of the 1980s. Violent crime peaked in the mid-1970s and again in the late 1980s, periods that saw a cross-party consensus in favor of mass incarceration. Since the early 1990s, homicide and virtually all categories of violent crime have fallen to roughly half the rate in the peak years of the late 1980s, even lower in some places.[11] A generation of Americans is coming of age and starting families without the horrifying sense that violent crime might engulf them. Along with other broad changes in the economy, this new, less fear-oriented sensibility is helping drive a major demographic trend in favor of cities and nearby suburbs with walkable access to parks and public transportation, a development considered utopian thinking in the 1980s and early 1990s.[12]

In the early 1990s, as the arc of mass incarceration was approaching its high noon, Malcolm Feeley and I described the rise of a "new penology" that pessimistically assumed the permanent nature of high crime levels and sought to manage crime down to an acceptable level by identifying high-risk populations for incapacitation.[13] Today, in marked contrast, a degree of optimism about crime prevention runs across the system. Great attention has been paid to more effective policing, especially in a few cities—including New York, Boston, and Los Angeles—with a credible claim to have implemented actual tactical changes.[14]

Less well known but also critical to transforming the common sense about crime prevention is the emergence of better strategies to treat people with serious mental illness. While a purely medical solution to serious mental illness remains in the future, intensive social services, provision of stable housing, and other aid programs have generated promising results in keeping people living with such illnesses out of emergency rooms and prisons.[15]

There's also reason for optimism about those being released from prison. In the mid-1990s, penologists began to rediscover *reentry*, that is, the idea that ex-cons might have trouble navigating the society from which they had been sequestered for years and that helping them find a job and a place to live might keep them from going back to a life of crime. Critiques of incapacitation systems, which simply dump former prisoners back into communities with little thought to prevent crime there, began to suggest that mass incarceration might be past its peak.[16] Today, accelerated to some degree by the recent Great Recession, many states are investing heavily in reentry strategies designed to drive down prison population through reduced recidivism. At the same time, a growing body of formerly incarcerated people are organizing to help others. The contrast with the 1970s could not be greater; both social scientists and former prisoners then rejected rehabilitation as a sham, and the first wave of empirical studies of police patrol tactics and parole and treatment strategies seemed to say, "Nothing works."

Another important source of change is the ascendance of dignity as a constitutional value within the legal system. As discussed, dignity has in recent decades become the conceptual engine of an emerging body of human rights law that in some regions, particularly Europe, has become a major influence on punishment and prisons. The United States, for historical reasons, had seemed largely indifferent to dignity, viewing it as adding little to existing constitutional values. However, in the last decade, the Supreme Court has been casting dignity in a stronger and more assertive role. *Brown v. Plata*, with its proclamation that "dignity animates the Eighth Amendment," is the most striking example thus far, and *Brown's* notion of dignity is particularly salient to punishment because it arises in a case that has essentially placed mass incarceration on trial.

This is not the first time American law has been influenced by the concept of dignity. During the cascade of human rights law started by the Universal Declaration of Human Rights in 1948, dignity as a source of human rights began to influence American constitutional law anew.[17] Arguments based on dignity emphasized the autonomy of the individual against the totalitarian state, the equal entitlement of all people to respect for their common humanity as against the horror of the Nazi's genocidal projects.

This first dignity wave had significant implications for punishment and for the confinement of people with mental illness. Influenced by concerns of autonomy and equality, the Supreme Court enhanced the rights of criminal defendants, especially the Fifth Amendment right to silence in *Miranda v. Arizona* (1966) and the Fourth Amendment right against "unreasonable searches and seizures" in *Mapp v. Ohio* (1961).[18] The Court also held that long-term hospitalization of people with mental illness who were receiving no treatment and posed no threat to themselves or others violated the due process clause of the Fourteenth and Fifth Amendments.[19] Federal courts also expanded protection for prisoners' rights under the Eighth Amendment.

Motivated by similar arguments, state legislatures in many states enacted reforms to involuntary hospitalization laws designed to limit long-term hospitalization, as well as sentencing reforms designed to end indeterminate prison sentences. Both reforms sprang from mistrust of expert-based systems of administrative discretion and instead favored liberty. Most of these reform efforts, however, had reached their conclusion by the 1980s. As state penal policies turned toward punishment and incapacitation, there was little in this first wave of dignity-based law reform to stem the tide. Many of these changes were intended to protect the autonomy of outpatients and those hospitalized or sentenced to rehabilitative prison sentences, but instead they contributed to the erosion of public confidence in the crime-suppressing capacities of the state. These reforms may now be seen in retrospect as feeding mass incarceration. That is why we must examine the crisis of mass incarceration for what dignity might mean as a legal value today. Mass incarceration is rotting from the inside. The penitentiary-style prison, designed to resist and treat diseases and injuries, has instead been proven to aggregate, exacerbate, and mismanage chronic illness. Mass incarceration turned the penitentiary into an even more hazardous and fundamentally unconstitutional institution by expanding the scale of imprisonment and reducing the capacity for individualized care.

The Eighth Amendment as it has been conventionally understood, however, is likely only to bite at the edges of such a system, condemning egregious failures in the delivery of essential services whose denial amounts to torture, or striking down the odd prison sentence, so wildly out of proportion to the underlying crime as to shock the conscience of a court. The question posed after *Brown v. Plata* is whether a dignity-animated Eighth Amendment will demand a more proactive and preventive criminal justice regime, one planned to prevent degrading conditions and proactively preserve the dignity of the incarcerated. The Supreme Court's recognition in *Brown* that state prison policies are subject to a politics that cannot be trusted to respect the humanity of prisoners gives lower courts a greater warrant to intervene.

Without such change, the future of American prisons holds frequent humanitarian crises and mounting challenges to the routine capacity of even decently managed prisons to protect the human dignity of prisoners as they age and diseases take their course.[20] Nor are these problems, stark as they are, likely to be containable to prisons and courts. Just as "jail disease" escaped its stigmatized frontline victims to become part of the broader burden of infectious disease facing urban populations in the late eighteenth and early nineteenth centuries, today chronic illness in prison endangers the fragile financing of health care for the poor outside prison walls. Although the nation cannot afford to continue on its present course, politicians will introduce substantial change only if they feel covered enough from the old charges of being soft on crime. California's prison health care crisis, the *Brown v. Plata* decision, and the new common sense about criminal justice emerging from them can help coalesce that kind of cultural change—but only if people know about prison conditions and act as if they matter.

Today the burden of proof remains on those of us calling for alternatives to prison; we must prove that they can work without a rise in crime. The old common sense remains, and the fact that the *Brown v. Plata* judges *accepted* that challenge and insisted that California could find nonprison alternatives for forty thousand convicted felons over two years without raising crime rates was important to demonstrating that dignity for prisoners does not come at the expense of dignity for victims of violent crime. But going forward, defenders of the status quo cannot be allowed to maintain decades-old assumptions about the blanket risks posed by incarcerated and criminalized populations.

States must undertake evaluation and public education. So far, California's elected leaders continue to discuss the prison crisis as a technical problem imposed on the state by the federal courts. Change must begin with remorse for a record of human rights violations that went on for decades and involved as many as a million Californians (not counting the prison officers). None of them was waterboarded, but many of them were subjected to torture on the installment plan, suffering as their chronic illnesses followed a predictable course as relief was withheld. We cannot move forward or reshape California's (or America's) broader crime prevention approach without acknowledging fault or the need for remorse and restoration.

One model that comes from transitional justice efforts around the globe is a "truth and reconciliation commission."[21] Under an immunity from prosecution or civil lawsuit, those officials who led us into mass incarceration, those who planned and operated prisons they knew would deny prisoners basic human rights such as health care, should be asked to testify why they felt justified in doing so. Under similar legal protections, the formerly incarcerated, especially those associated with prison gangs, should testify as to the way incarceration has influenced their criminal careers, the purpose of prison gangs, and how their members can be reintegrated into the community.

The reach of human rights norms as a counterweight to punitive populism in Europe owes much to the development of specialized governmental organs to support this mission. The Committee for the Prevention of Torture and the Committee of Ministers of the Council of Europe each bring different kinds of expertise and authority to the protection of human rights for those imprisoned, at once augmenting and informing the courts. The United States as a whole and especially the states that lead in incarceration need to establish similar agencies whose rules and inspections can shape a criminal justice bureaucracy that will be a positive force for protecting human rights in prison rather than the negative force it has been in California. Given the state's history of confinement and human rights abuses among the confined, as well as its record of trying to stop courts from using their powers to find and condemn abuse, California needs affirmative measures to prevent future fear-based policies from producing degrading and inhumane treatment.

Finally, we need to consider amending our state constitutions and the United States Constitution so that our central norms against excessive and abusive treatment and punishment are modernized to address the now-recognized threats of mass incarceration. The easiest and most direct route would be to adopt the language of the Universal Declaration of Human Rights, Article 5.1:

> No one shall be subjected to torture or to cruel, inhuman or degrading treatment or punishment.

In 1948, when the United States became one of the original signing nations, legal experts on both sides of the Atlantic assumed that these words meant largely the same thing as the Eighth Amendment's ban on "cruel and unusual punishment." Indeed during the 1960s and 1970s, the United States was advancing prisoners' rights under the Eighth Amendment further than European member states were under the European Convention on Human Rights. However since the 1980s, the United States has followed a different trajectory, along which the modern ideas of dignity implicit in the language of Article 5.1 and explicit in the preamble of the Declaration were largely abandoned in the name of security from violent crime at any price. Since then, the two sides of the Atlantic seemed to reverse their stances, U.S. courts bowing low to mass incarceration while European human rights law instituted a wide variety of normative requirements on member states, from prison health care to prisoner voting.[22]

Brown v. Plata suggests that a slender majority of the Supreme Court would like to move Eighth Amendment law back closer to the interpretive trajectory that Europeans have taken. If dignity indeed "animates" the amendment, many of the same considerations should arise. But Supreme Court majorities are notoriously fickle, and memories fade of the social circumstances that necessitated great constitutional changes in interpretation. If Americans in this generation come to feel, as I do, that mass incarceration belongs among our collection of profound aberrations from our democracy—including slavery, Jim Crow, the treatment of Native Americans, the internment of Japanese Americans during World War II, and the warehousing of thousands of people with mental illnesses throughout the twentieth century—we will need to change the Constitution to make sure future generations avoid repeating our mistakes.

Adopting the language of Article Five of the Universal Declaration of Human Rights as an alternative or a supplement to the Eighth Amendment's language on cruel and unusual punishment would have several long-term consequences for prisons and their jurisprudence. First, the view long held by some justices that the clause protects only against torture would be permanently repudiated, for the new language includes torture but clearly extends to forbid punishments that are degrading and inhuman as well as cruel. Second, by using *cruel* without its seventeenth-century companion, *unusual*, the new language would invite courts to expand the Eighth Amendment's proportionality principle, under which only a very tiny number of excessive prison sentences have ever been set aside as disproportionate.

Finally, by mentioning treatment as well as punishment, the language of the provision would escape numerous formalistic precedents in which the Supreme Court has held the Eighth Amendment irrelevant to civil forms of detention, including immigration and punitive civil commitment programs, such as the "violent sexual predator programs" that operate in some sixteen states and that are currently beyond the reach of the Eighth Amendment on the ground that they are instances of civil detention rather than punishment.

Like Noah's children, we stand just after the high-water mark of an epic flood of imprisonment, a flood that drowned whole communities and harmed and disabled millions over the course of decades. As the waters recede, those with power will quickly define the wreckage left behind in society as beyond the scope of reasonable reform. Already the safe line for politicians appears to be in favor of "evidence-based alternatives" meant to save money while keeping crime low. While surely this is better than reckless imprisonment, it does little to reduce the senseless fear of crime or reduce the stigma heaped on the formerly incarcerated. Mass imprisonment must end. It endangers human dignity. It is a violation of human rights and international law. It is unconstitutional. It does not protect public safety. The human dignity of prisoners, exposed by the shocking and degrading conditions in California's prisons, provides our best guide going forward as we reimagine criminal justice institutions that can protect safety, provide justice for victims, and respect the decency of a civilized society.

Notes

Introduction: Inhuman Punishment

1. Indeed, 2010 was the first year in the last thirty-seven in which the nationwide prison population decreased. See "Total Correctional Population" and subpages at www.bjs.gov/index.cfm?ty=tp &tid=11; and Paul Guerino, Paige M. Harrison, and William J. Sabol, *Prisoners in 2010*, rev ed. (Washington, DC: Bureau of Justice Statistics, 2011), www.bjs.gov/index.cfm?ty=pbdetail&iid=2230.

2. Bruce Western and Becky Pettit have calculated that for men born between 1975 and 1979, more than 5 percent of whites and 25 percent of blacks will serve time in prison before the end of their lives. For many this will mean a lifetime of legal prohibitions to work in certain fields, to vote, and to serve on juries. See Bruce Western and Becky Pettit, "Incarceration and Social Inequality," *Daedalus* 139, no. 3 (Summer 2010): 8–19.

3. The research is there, but it has yet to reach the kind of public awareness that the quantitative dimension of mass incarceration has. See Benjamin Fleury Steiner with Carla Crowder, *Dying on the Inside: The HIV/AIDs Ward at Limestone Prison* (Ann Arbor: University of Michigan Press, 2008); and Sharon Dolovich, "Cruelty, Prison Conditions and the Eighth Amendment," *New York Law Review* 84, no. 4 (2009): 881.

4. William Stuntz, *The Collapse of American Criminal Justice* (Cambridge, MA: Harvard University Press, 2012).

5. Jonathan Simon, *Poor Discipline: Parole and the Social Control of the Underclass, 1890–1990* (Chicago: University of Chicago Press, 1997).

6. Franklin E. Zimring and Gordon Hawkins, *The Scale of Imprisonment* (Chicago: University of Chicago Press, 1991); see also David Garland, "Introduction: The Meaning of Mass Imprisonment," in *Mass Imprisonment: Social Causes and Consequences* (London: Sage, 2001), 1–3.

7. Bruce Western, *Punishment and Inequality in America* (New York: Russell Sage Foundation, 2006).

8. Todd R. Clear, *Imprisoning Communities: How Mass Incarceration Makes Disadvantaged Neighborhoods Worse* (New York: Oxford University Press, 2007).

9. Franklin Zimring, *The Great American Crime Decline* (New York: Oxford University Press, 2006).

10. Marie Gottschalk, "Cell Blocks & Red Ink: Mass Incarceration, the Great Recession & Penal Reform," *Daedalus* 139, no. 3 (Summer 2010): 62–73.

11. *Spain v. Procunier*, 600 F.2d 189 (1979).

12. As before, this is only to note the quantitative dimension. The qualitative features of who is incarcerated and how also factor into the inhumanity of our practices.

13. There have been important exceptions. See especially James Q. Whitman, *Harsh Justice: Criminal Punishment and the Widening Divide Between America and Europe* (New York: Oxford University Press, 2003); and Fleury-Steiner with Crowder, *Dying Inside*.

14. Ethan Blue, "The Strange Career of Leo Stanley: Remaking Manhood and Medicine at San Quentin State Penitentiary, 1913–1951," *Pacific Historical Review* 78, no. 2 (May 2009): 210–41.

15. Malcolm Feeley and Edward Rubin, *Judicial Policy Making and the Modern State: How the Courts Reformed America's Prisons* (Cambridge: Cambridge University Press, 1998).

16. The special court was required by the Prison Litigation Reform Act, the goal being to make reform orders involving state prisons harder to achieve and specifically to make population limits on prisons very difficult to establish.

17. Coleman-Plata v. Schwarzenegger, U.S. District Court, E.D. and N. D. Cal., Three-Judge Court Pursuant to 28 U.S.C. § 2284,

No. CIV S-90-0520 LKK JFM P and No. C01-1351 TEH, www.caed
.uscourts.gov/caed/Documents/90cv520010804.pdf.

18. Brown v. Plata, 131 S.Ct. 1910, 1928.

19. Brown v. Plata, 563 U.S. (2011).

20. Ibid., Alito dissent at 17.

21. Alexander, *New Jim Crow.*

22. See Rebecca McClennan, *The Crisis of Imprisonment: Protest, Politics and the Making of the American Penal State, 1776–1941* (New York: Cambridge University Press, 2008).

23. David Garland may be correct in saying that the "culture of control" is founded in a new "common sense of high crime societies," but it was very specific crimes and contexts that figured in the publicized crime panics of that decade. David Garland, *The Culture of Control: Crime and Social Order in Contemporary Society* (Chicago: University of Chicago Press, 2001).

24. Jonathan Simon, "Total Incapacitation: The Penal Imaginary and the Rise of an Extreme Penal Rationale in California in the 1970s," in *Incapacitation: Trends and New Perspectives,* ed. Marijke Malsch and Marius Duker (Farnham, UK: Ashgate, 2012).

25. Sharon Shalev, *Supermax: Controlling Risk Through Solitary Confinement* (London: Willan, 2009).

26. Keramet Reiter, "The Most Restrictive Alternative: The Origins, Functions, Control and Ethical Implications of the Supermax Prison, 1976–2010," PhD diss., University of California–Berkeley School of Law, 2012.

27. Coleman v. Wilson, 912 F.Supp. 1282 (E.D. Cal. 1995), rbgg .com/wp-content/uploads/Coleman-v-Wilson-912-F-Supp-1282 -ED-Cal-1995.pdf.

28. *Coleman* implicitly raises the question of how many of these prisoners would even be incarcerated at all but for the presence of assertive imprisonment policies and the absence of an effective system of mental health care, thereby challenging the axiom that incapacitation must promote public safety.

29. Plata v. Davis stipulation for Injunctive Relief (N.D. Cal. 2002, stipulated agreement), www.clearinghouse.net/chDocs /public/PC-CA-0018-0005.pdf.

30. In most of the cases discussed the prisoners were represented by the Prison Law Office and lawyers Donald Specter, Steven Fama, and Sara Norman, as well as a variety of other firms

and organizations including lawyers Michael Bien and Ernest Galvan. In what follows I rely on the judicial decisions that emerged from this litigation. If these cases are as a significant as I believe, there will be time to tell the story of these lawyers and the extraordinary collaboration with California prisoners to put the state's extreme mass incarceration system on trial.

31. The PLRA created a number of new procedural obstacles for prisoners seeking to challenge state prison policies in court, especially if the resulting order might require states to release prisoners or not accept them.

32. Ian Loader and Richard Sparks, *Public Criminology?* (New York: Routledge, 2010).

1. Total Incapacitation: The 1970s and the Birth of an Extreme Penology

1. Franklin E. Zimring, Gordon Hawkins, and Sam Kamin, *Punishment and Democracy: Three Strikes and You're Out in California* (New York: Oxford University Press, 2003).

2. Tim Newburn, "Diffusion, Differentiation and Resistance in Comparative Penality," *Criminology & Criminal Justice* 10, no. 4 (November 2010): 341–52, fig. 2, p. 349.

3. Franklin Zimring, *The Great American Crime Decline* (New York: Oxford University Press, 2006).

4. Jonathan Simon, "Mass Incarceration: From Social Policy, to Politics, to Problem," in *The Oxford Handbook of Sentencing and Corrections*, ed. Kevin Reitz and Joan Petersilia (New York: Oxford University Press, 2012), 23–52; William A. Fischel, "Homevoters, Municipal Corporate Governance, and the Benefit View of the Property Tax," *National Tax Journal* 54, no. 1 (2001).

5. Todd Gitlin's inspiring memoir of the 1960s gives me my counterpoint. See Todd Gitlin, *The 1960s: Years of Hope, Days of Rage* (New York: Bantam, 1993).

6. Joan Didion, *Where I Was From* (New York: Vintage, 2003).

7. David Garland, *The Culture of Control: Crime and Social Order in Contemporary Society* (Chicago: University of Chicago Press, 2001).

8. Mona Lynch, *Sunbelt Justice: Arizona and the Transformation of American Punishment* (Palo Alto, CA: Stanford University Press, 2009); and Joshua Page, *The Toughest Beat: Politics, Punishment, and*

the Prison Officers Union in the United States (New York: Oxford University Press, 2010).

9. Ian Loader and Richard Sparks, *Public Criminology?* (New York: Routledge, 2010); Garland, *Culture of Control*; and John Pratt, *Penal Populism* (New York: Routledge, 2007).

10. Zimring et al., *Punishment and Democracy*; and Vanessa Barker, *The Politics of Imprisonment: How the Democratic Process Shapes the Way America Punishes Offenders* (New York: Oxford University Press, 2009).

11. The shifting sources of prison population growth in California since the start of mass incarceration are charted in Franklin E. Zimring, "Penal Policy and Penal Legislation in Recent American Experience," *Stanford Law Review* 58 (2005): 323.

12. Zimring et al., *Punishment and Democracy*.

13. Charles Taylor, *Modern Social Imaginaries* (Durham, NC: Duke University Press, 2003), 22.

14. Ibid., 24.

15. An influential example was Howard Becker, *The Outsiders: Studies in the Sociology of Deviance* (New York: The Free Press, 1963).

16. Gresham Sykes, *Society of Captives: A Study of a Maximum Security Prison* (Princeton, NJ: Princeton University Press, 1958).

17. A taste of that support was reflected in the legislative adoption of a prisoners' bill of rights in 1975; see "Senate Panel Passes Bill to Repeal Prisoners Bill of Rights," *Los Angeles Times*, April 5, 1994.

18. Eric Cummins, *The Rise and Fall of California's Radical Prison Movement* (Palo Alto, CA: Stanford University Press, 1996).

19. That threat of life was the formal meaning of California's Indeterminate Sentence Law, under which Jackson was sentenced, along with nearly all Californians convicted of felonies from 1944 through 1976. Crimes carried terms such as six months to life, with the administrative "Adult Authority" responsible for setting a presumptive release date based on rehabilitative considerations and subject to revision. In practice the system seems to have operated on rough guidelines that gave little heed to individual factors but could easily be varied in a case like Jackson's where the individual prisoner was viewed as an enemy of prison authority. See Sheldon Messinger and Philip Johnson, "California's Determinate Sentencing Statute: History and Issues," in *Determinate Sentencing: Reform or Regression?* Proceedings of the Special Conference on Determinate Sentencing, June 2–3, 1977, National Institute of Law

Enforcement and Criminal Justice, Law Enforcement Assistance Administration (Washington, DC: U.S. Department of Justice, 1978), 15–17.

20. Spain v. Rushen, 883 F.2d 712 (1989).

21. Cummins, *Rise and Fall*, 213.

22. Heather Thompson, "The Lingering Injustice of Attica," *New York Times*, September 8, 2011, A31.

23. Indeed, nearly forty years after his death, the image of George Jackson continues to haunt the organizational core of corrections in California. In 2004 when former gang leader–turned–antigang author Stanley "Tookie" Williams faced execution at San Quentin and received unusually broad support for clemency from politicians and the media, Governor Schwarzenegger's denial of clemency specifically cited Williams's identification with George Jackson as evidence of his lack of reform.

24. Page, *Toughest Beat*; Katherine Beckett, *Making Crime Pay: Law and Order in Contemporary American Politics* (New York: Oxford University Press, 1997).

25. John Irwin, *Prisons in Turmoil* (Boston: Little, Brown, 1980).

26. James Alan Fox and Jack Levin, *Extreme Killing: Understanding Serial and Mass Murder* (Thousand Oaks, CA: Sage, 2005).

27. The genre of movies graphically depicting psychopathic killers has roots as far back as the 1930s but did not really become established until the 1970s, when they became one of Hollywood's most potent and enduring formulas. They continue to enjoy a steady audience today, but the peak may have come in 1983 when nearly 60 percent of ticket sales were accounted for by slasher films. See "Slasher Film," Wikipedia, www.wikipedia.org/wiki/Slasher_film. The brand has continued in more ironic form in such acclaimed contemporary television series as *The Wire* (season 5), and *Dexter*.

28. People v. Anderson, 493 P.2d 880, 6 Cal. 3d 628 (Cal. 1972).

29. Charles Manson and his "family" were perhaps the most enduring symbol of evil to emerge from the late 1960s. The horribly bloody murders of Sharon Tate and four other people at the posh house she shared with Roman Polanski in the hills above Hollywood in August 1969 and the equally bloody murders of Leno and Rosemary LaBianca in a more urban but still very comfortable and secure neighborhood a week later, sent all of Los Angeles and much of the world into a frenzy of fear. Manson and his

followers have been the direct subject of dozens of movies and an inspiration for key elements in scores more, so the horror remains alive even as the key players age and die after four solid decades of incarceration. Ed Sanders, *The Family* (New York: Thunder's Mouth Press, 2002).

30. As an alternative to incarceration as well as a form of control and treatment administered by the state's mental health system.

31. Malcolm Feeley and Edward Rubin, *Judicial Policy Making and the Modern State: How the Courts Reformed America's Prisons* (Cambridge: Cambridge University Press, 1998).

32. Ewing v. California, 538 U.S. 11 (2003).

33. Michael Tonry, ed., *Retributivism Has a Past: Has It a Future?* (New York: Oxford University Press, 2011).

34. See American Friends Service Committee, *Struggle for Justice: A Report on Crime and Punishment in America* (New York: Farrar, Straus and Giroux, 1971); Andrew von Hirsch, *Doing Justice: The Choice of Punishments* (New York: Hill & Wang, 1974).

35. Franklin Zimring and Gordon Hawkins, *Incapacitation: Penal Confinement and the Restraint of Crime* (New York: Oxford University Press, 1995).

36. Ibid., 4, emphasis in original.

37. Zimring et al., *Punishment and Democracy*; Ruth Gilmore, *Golden Gulag: Prisons, Surplus, Crisis, and Opposition in Globalizing California* (Berkeley: University of California Press, 2007); Page, *Toughest Beat*.

38. Zimring and Hawkins, *Incapacitation*, 15.

39. As Zimring and Hawkins point out, the former is much more compatible with a stable or even shrinking prison population, while the latter almost inevitably leads to growth in prison populations. Ibid., 12.

40. Law students learn that imprisonment is only loosely related to the specific acts a person has committed, because modern penal codes contain so many crimes with very different levels of punishment, and prosecutors have discretion to charge any crime whose elements can be proven by the evidence.

41. Zimring et al., *Punishment and Democracy*.

42. Thus incapacitation as the primary penal purpose did not even exclude other security messages from becoming part of the general common sense of the 1970s in California. Other features of that message included: gated communities (you should live in as

physically secure an environment as possible); firearms (you need to protect your shelter against those who get past the gate); and capital punishment (the existence of which helps assure that instant permanent incapacitation is the real sanction for those whose high risk of repeated lethal violence has been demonstrated).

43. Zimring and Hawkins, *Incapacitation*, 16, emphasis in original.

44. Ibid., 75.

45. Gilmore, *Golden Gulag*.

46. Zimring and Hawkins, *Incapacitation*, 172.

47. Probably the foremost defender of the incapacitative effects of mass incarceration is economist Steven Levitt, but even he does not necessarily defend current levels of incarceration as optimal. See Steven D. Levitt and Stephen J. Dubner, *Freakonomics: A Rogue Economist Explores the Hidden Side of Everything* (New York: William Morrow, 2009), ch. 3.

48. Zimring, *Great American Crime Decline*; Franklin Zimring, *The City That Became Safe: New York's Lessons for Crime and Its Control* (New York: Oxford University Press, 2012).

2. The House of Fear: Dignity and Risk in Madrid v. Gomez

1. Sharon Shalev, *Supermax: Controlling Risk Through Solitary Confinement* (London: Willan, 2009), 3, 4, 225; Keramet Reiter, "The Most Restrictive Alternative: The Origins, Functions, Control and Ethical Implications of the Supermax Prison, 1976–2010," PhD diss., University of California–Berkeley School of Law, 2012.

2. Between 1995 and 2000, while the overall prison population increased 28 percent, the number of prisoners housed in segregation units increased by 40 percent. The Commission on Safety and Abuse in America's Prisons, *Confronting Confinement* (New York: Vera Institute of Justice, 2006), 53.

3. Madrid v. Gomez, 889 F.Supp. 1146 (N.D. Cal. 1995).

4. Gustave De Beaumont and Alexis de Tocqueville, *On the Penitentiary System in the United States and Its Application in France* (Philadelphia: Carey, 1833); Charles Dickens, *American Notes* (1842); John Howard, *The State of the Prisons in England and Wales* (Warrington, UK: William Eyres, 1777; 2d ed., 1789).

5. *Madrid*, 889 F.Supp. at 1265.

6. Shalev, *Supermax*, 22; Reiter, "Most Restrictive Alternative" (PhD diss.).

7. The Adjustment Center takeover is discussed in detail in the previous chapter. It is only a slight exaggeration to say that almost everything that has happened in California prisons since the 1980s was a response to the events of that single day and the way they have come to be remembered inside the prison bureaucracy. Ultimately the new Correctional Officers Union built itself into a powerhouse of legislative support for prison expansion; see Joshua Page, *The Toughest Beat: Politics, Punishment, and the Prison Officers Union in California* (New York: Oxford University Press, 2010).

8. Spain v. Procunier, 600 F.2d 189, 196 (1979).

9. Keramet Ann Reiter, "The Most Restrictive Alternative: A Litigation History of Solitary Confinement in U.S. Prisons, 1960–2006," in *Studies in Law, Politics, and Society*, vol. 57, ed. Austin Sarat (Bingley, UK: Emerald Group Publishing Limited, 2012), 71–124.

10. The court concluded that the factual record did not demonstrate such a climate. There was little analysis of double-celling in the supermax context.

11. "Illegal" is an administrative determination by the California Department of Corrections and Rehabilitation, which classifies these groups as "security threat groups." Being validated as an associate of one of these gangs is grounds for being held in the SHU indefinitely.

12. Not incidentally in *Spain v. Procunier* itself.

13. Ironies and historical connections abound here. The district court decision in *Spain* may have been one of the factors that convinced CDC administrators that they needed new purpose-built security prisons to withstand judicial scrutiny. Meanwhile in 1988, Judge Thelton Henderson (who would conduct the *Madrid* trial in 1994) ordered Johnny Spain to receive a new criminal trial based on procedural errors. He was subsequently acquitted and never went back to prison.

14. *Madrid*, 889 F.Supp. at 1227.

15. Ironically, including Johnny Spain himself, who replaced George Jackson as the most feared prisoner in the system and, along with the other survivors of the AC takeover, became the model targets of the SHU.

16. Statement of Betty Bianca, wife of a hunger striker incarcerated in the SHU during a press conference in front of the *Los*

Angeles Times, August 7, 2013. "There are no serial killers in the SHU. There are no rapists or child molesters in the SHU." "Challenging CDCR Secretary Jeffrey Beard's Disinformation and Lies Targeting the CA Prisoner Hunger Strike to Stop Solitary Confinement Torture," Stop Mass Incarceration in the Bay Area, August 8, 2013, stopmassincarcerationbayarea.tumblr.com/post/576840337 72/challenging-cdcr-secretary-jeffrey-beards.

17. Shalev, *Supermax*, 71; Reiter, "Most Restrictive Alternative."

18. Other states have filled them with a mix of others. Prisoners who commit serious violent crimes inside prisons are also obvious candidates, as are those whose conflict with other prisoners is visible enough to anticipate that a violent crime or widespread prison disruption is likely to occur. To these can be added a number of inmates who are deemed candidates for protection because they have committed a very unpopular sort of crime (like child rape) or are presumed to have provided information to prison officers (snitches). Some states (e.g., Arizona) have rounded this out by placing their death row in a supermax.

19. The full history of the post-1970s gang system in California has yet to be written. The gangs' origin lies in the racial identity groups that emerged from the violent fallout of the once unifying prisoner-rights movement. See John Irwin, *Prisons in Turmoil* (New York: Little, Brown, 1980) for a detailed account of California prisons at this conjuncture.

20. The practice of racial assignment in cells was held by the Supreme Court to be a form of racial classification subject to strict scrutiny in California v. Johnson, 543 U.S. 499 (2005). The state would presumably have defended the necessity for such assignment and lockdowns on a racial basis for security but instead negotiated a settlement of the case.

21. Even this latter part varies in certain contexts, such as the forestry camps and the education centers.

22. Reiter, "Most Restrictive Alternative," 161.

23. Wolff v. McDonnell, 418 U.S. 539 (1974).

24. Helms v. Hewitt, 459 U.S. 460, 103 S.Ct. 864, 74 L.Ed.2d 675 (1983).

25. *Madrid*, 889 F.Supp. at 1244 (quotations in original).

26. Davis was convicted of kidnapping a twelve-year-old girl from her home and murdering her. Having served previously in prison, he became the focus of the campaign to enact the state's

extreme version of three strikes in 1994. See Franklin E. Zimring, Gordon Hawkins, and Sam Kamin, *Punishment and Democracy: Three Strikes and You're Out in California* (New York: Oxford University Press, 2003).

27. Michelle Brown, *The Culture of Punishment: Prison, Society, and Spectacle* (New York: New York University Press, 2009).

28. Which results in many supermax prisoners being released at the completion of their sentence directly from the SHU without any period of transition or reentry program into the general population. Reiter, "Most Restrictive Alternative."

29. Pieter Spierenberg, *The Spectacle of Suffering: Executions and the Evolution of Repression* (Cambridge: Cambridge University Press, 1984).

30. *Madrid*, 889 F.Supp. at 1172.

31. KQED News, "Judge Closes Prison Abuse Case After 20 Years," March 22, 2011, blogs.kqed.org/newsfix/2011/03/22/judge-closes-prison-abuse-case-after-20-years/.

32. *Madrid*, 889 F.Supp. at 1214.

33. Keramet Reiter's research indicates that CDC administrators were given virtually total discretion to decide what kinds of facilities to build and that they took their time to carefully assess what they wanted, visiting numerous states before settling on Arizona's pioneering ADX supermax.

34. *Madrid*, 889 F.Supp. at 1218.

35. Ibid., 1217.

36. Ibid., 1220.

37. Ibid., 1221.

38. Ibid., 1261.

39. Touissaint v. McCarthy, 801 F.2d 1080 (9th Cir. 1986). This important litigation was one of the first nationwide to challenge the penal practices associated with California's shift away from its treatment model to the monopoly of incapacitation and eventually mass incarceration.

40. *Madrid*, 889 F.Supp. at 1262.

41. Terry Kupers, "Two Steps Forward, One Step Back," *California Prison Focus*, no. 21 (Fall 2004): 3.

42. The state announced a modest reform in its policies to permit prisoners to gradually "step down" from SHU custody without the previous requirement of debriefing, but it offers little immediate promise of an exit. In June 2013, the three-judge court

rebuffed efforts by the governor to terminate the population-cap order at close to the 145 percent of capacity that the state originally sought in the *Plata* case. The state is appealing.

43. *Madrid*, 889 F.Supp. 1146, 1263.

44. Giorgio Agamben, *Homo Sacer: Sovereign Power and Bare Life*, trans. Daniel Heller-Roazen (Palo Alto, CA: Stanford University Press, 1998).

3. *Engines of Madness:* Coleman v. Wilson

1. Coleman v. Wilson, 912 F.Supp. 1282, 1298 (E.D. Cal. 1995), rbgg.com/wp-content/uploads/Coleman-v-Wilson-912-F-Supp -1282-ED-Cal-1995.pdf.

2. Texas is the clearest example; see Robert Perkinson, *Texas Tough: The Rise of America's Prison Empire* (New York: Picador, 2010); and Michael Berryhill, *The Trials of Eroy Brown: The Murder Case That Shook the Texas Prison System* (Austin: University of Texas Press, 2012). Arizona is another; see Mona Lynch, *Sunbelt Justice: Arizona and the Transformation of American Punishment* (Palo Alto, CA: Stanford University Press, 2010).

3. Michel Foucault, *The History of Madness*, trans. Jean Khalfa (New York: Routledge, 2006); and David J. Rothman, *The Discovery of the Asylum* (Boston: Little, Brown, 1972).

4. John Sutton, *Stubborn Children: Controlling Delinquency in the United States, 1640–1981* (Berkeley: University of California Press, 1993); David Garland, *Punishment and Welfare: A History of Penal Strategies* (Farnham, UK: Gower, 1985); and David Rothman, *Conscience and Convenience: The Asylum and Its Alternatives in Progressive America* (Piscataway, NJ: Aldine Transaction, 2002).

5. Most of these sentences are reduced at a standard rate for time served without disciplinary violations.

6. Most other states did not follow California as far in embracing retribution and determinate sentences, but indifference to individual psychology was widespread, even in states that retained the legal forms of indeterminate sentencing, parole, and rehabilitation.

7. William Stuntz, *The Collapse of American Criminal Justice* (Cambridge, MA: Harvard University Press, 2011).

8. Paul Appelbaum, *Almost a Revolution: Mental Health Law and the Limits of Change* (New York: Oxford University Press, 1994).

9. Empirical research on the relationship at the state level between changes in the populations of the mental hospitals and the prisons showed no relationship during the first thirty years of deinstitutionalization, from 1950 to 1980, but between 1980 and 2000, deinstitutionalization accounted for 4 to 7 percent of incarceration growth. See Steven Raphael and Michael Stoll, "Assessing the Contribution of the Deinstitutionalization of the Mentally Ill to Growth in the U.S. Incarceration Rate," *Journal of Legal Studies* 42, no. 1 (2013): 187–222.

10. John Monahan, Henry Steadman, Eric Silver, Paul Appelbaum, Pamela Clark Robbins, Edward Mulvey, Lauren Roth, Thomas Grisso, and Stephen Banks, *Rethinking Risk Assessment: The MacArthur Study of Mental Disorder and Violence* (New York: Oxford University Press, 2001).

11. *Coleman,* 912 F.Supp. at 1299.

12. Ibid., 1306.

13. As this book goes to press, Judge Karlton is considering new Eighth Amendment claims by advocates for prisoners focusing on California's heavy reliance on physical force, including with the use of special weapons, to manage prisoners with serious mental illnesses.

14. Ibid., 1309.

15. Brown v. Plata, 131 S.Ct. 1920, 1928.

16. David Garland, *The Culture of Control: Crime and Social Order in Contemporary Society* (Chicago: University of Chicago Press, 2002), 11.

17. *Coleman,* 912 F.Supp. at 1315.

18. Ibid., 1317.

19. Ibid., 1319.

20. See Michel Foucault, *Discipline and Punish: The Birth of the Prison,* trans. Alan Sheridan (New York: Pantheon, 1977). In his influential genealogy of the modern prison, written while the rehabilitative model still held sway over most state prison systems and in Europe, the late philosopher, historian, and prisoner-rights activist Michel Foucault described the prison uprisings of the late 1960s and early 1970s, especially San Quentin and Attica, as nothing short of a rebellion anchored in the soul against this specific regime of penal control. Foucault, who died in 1984, never commented on the emerging mass-incarceration regime, but he would have appreciated the irony that it was courts that returned the soul to the prison.

4. Torture on the Installment Plan: Prisons Without
Medicine in Plata v. Davis

1. Estelle v. Gamble, 429 U.S. 97 (1976).
2. Brie Williams, James S. Goodwin, Jacques Baillargeon, Cyrus Ahalt, and Louise C. Walter, "Addressing the Aging Crisis in US Criminal Justice Health Care, *Journal of the American Geriatrics Association* 60 (2012): 1160.
3. Legal mechanisms to parole or commute the sentences of such prisoners existed, but the logic of total incapacitation, discussed in chapter 2, prevented the state from utilizing them.
4. Making it arguably the largest prisoner lawsuit in the history of the world.
5. Plata v. Davis, No. C1-3051, TEH, United States District Court for the Northern District of California, Complaint, 2.
6. Ibid., 4.
7. Ibid., 7.
8. Ibid., 10.
9. Ibid., 13.
10. The parties began negotiating about the needed reforms in 1999, two years before the lawsuit was filed.
11. Plata v. Davis, No. 3:01-cv-01351 (N.D. Cal. Apr. 5, 2001; now denominated Plata v. Brown).
12. Plata v. Schwarzenegger, Findings of Fact and Conclusions of Law Re Appointment of a Receiver, No. C1-3051, TEH, United States District Court for the Northern District of California, Oct. 3, 2005, 27.
13. Ibid., 44.
14. Franklin Zimring, "Penal Policy and Penal Legislation: Recent American Experience," *Stanford Law Review* 58, no. 1 (October 2005): 323–38.
15. Plata v. Schwarzenegger, Findings of Fact and Conclusions of Law Re Appointment of a Receiver, 8.
16. Ibid., 24.
17. This has become painfully obvious to California at a time of enormous revenue declines due to the economic recession. Judge Henderson was aghast in his receivership order that the "Department's annual health care budget has risen to over $1 billion"; by 2010 that was $2 billion. Within that gargantuan budget, a growing portion is accounted for by the costs of chronic illnesses and the

specialty medical services they require as they advance, amounting to a quarter of the correctional budget, or $500 million dollars, by 2010. Inevitably, those near death of advanced chronic illness use up an extraordinary portion of health resources while their quality of life deteriorates. In 2010 the sickest 1,200 prisoners in the California prison system were drawing $185 million in specialty medical services on top of the nearly $2.5 billion the state spends for its in-house correctional health care. See California State Auditor, California Department of Corrections and Rehabilitation, *Inmates Sentenced Under the Three Strikes Law and a Small Number of Inmates Receiving Specialty Health Care Represent Significant Costs*, May 2010, Report 2009-107.2, iv.

18. Plata v. Schwarzenegger, Findings of Fact and Conclusions of Law Re Appointment of a Receiver, 20–21.

19. To paraphrase Clausewitz's famous formula regarding war.

20. Plata v. Schwarzenegger, Findings of Fact and Conclusions of Law Re Appointment of a Receiver, 6.

21. Ibid., 15.

22. Ibid., 22.

23. As Joe Sim showed in his classic study of the Prison Health Service in England, medical authorities had long adopted disciplinary and punitive goals and been coopted by custodial personnel. But while English prison health reflects an overly close relationship between medical professionals and custody staff, the California story is one of hostility and subordination. See Joe Sim, *Medical Power in Prisons: The Prison Medical Service in England, 1774–1989* (London: Open University Press, 1990).

24. Ibid.

25. Ibid., 25.

26. Ibid., 9–10.

27. Howard, the once-sickly son of a wealthy family of intense religious values, was captured by French privateers on his way to help victims of the 1755 Lisbon earthquake, was moved by the conditions he witnessed in French jails, and on his release campaigned on behalf of captured seamen. Later, he turned a hereditary role as a local sheriff into an opportunity to inspect jails and other detention facilities throughout England and Scotland. His detailed notes, published in 1777 as *The State of the Prisons in England and Wales*, focused a great deal on the disease-inducing

qualities of confinement, especially lack of ventilation. A second edition was published posthumously with an extended new section on "the principal lazarettos of Europe." Howard completed the research before dying of disease he likely acquired visiting jails. See generally Michael Meranze, *Laboratories of Virtue: Punishment, Revolution, and Authority in Philadelphia, 1780–1830* (Chapel Hill: University of North Carolina Press, 1996).

28. Sim, *Medical Power in Prisons*.

29. I do not mean to discount the importance of other influences, such as workhouses and asylums, but only to highlight the impact of concerns about disease on key features of almost all the prison designs that followed.

30. Meranze, *Laboratories of Virtue*.

31. The late philosopher Michel Foucault drew on Bentham's design to characterize the disciplinary logic supporting the rise of the prison. See Michel Foucault, *Discipline and Punish: The Birth of the Prison*, trans. Alan Sheridan (New York: Pantheon, 1977).

32. Jeremy Bentham, *Panopticon; or, The Inspection-House* (London: 1787, 1791), Letter VII, *The Panopticon Writings*, ed. Miran Bozovic (London: Verso, 2011), cartome.org/panopticon2.htm#VII.

33. Malcolm Feeley and Edward Rubin, *Judicial Policy Making and the Modern State* (Cambridge: Cambridge University Press, 1998).

34. Estelle v. Gamble, 429 U.S. 97 (1976).

35. Rod Morgan, "Developing Prison Standards Compared," *Punishment and Society* 2, no. 3 (2000): 325–42.

36. Spain v. Procunier, 600 F.2d 189, 193 (CA9 1979).

37. Plata v. Schwarzenegger, Findings of Fact and Conclusions of Law Re Appointment of a Receiver, 48, quoting William Fletcher, "The Discretionary Constitution," *Yale Law Journal*, 1981.

38. Plata v. Schwarzenegger, Findings of Fact and Conclusions of Law Re Appointment of Receiver, 4.

5. Places of Extreme Peril: Coleman-Plata v. Schwarzenegger *and California's Prisons in the Era of Chronic Hyper-Overcrowding*

1. Coleman-Plata v. Schwarzenegger, U.S. District Court, E.D. and N.D. Cal., Three-Judge Court Pursuant to 28 U.S.C. § 2284, No. CIV S-90-0520 LKK JFM P and No. C01-1351 TEH, Opinion and

Order, August 4, 2009, www.caed.uscourts.gov/caed/Documents
/90cv520010804.pdf, 6.

2. Mona Lynch, *Sunbelt Justice: Arizona and the Transformation of
American Punishment* (Palo Alto, CA: Stanford University Press,
2009).

3. Jonathan Simon, *Governing Through Crime* (New York: Oxford University Press, 2009), chap. 2.

4. Sheldon L. Messinger, John E. Berecochea, David Rauma,
and Richard A. Berk, "Foundations of Parole in California," *Law
and Society Review* 19 (1985), no. 1: 69–106.

5. *Coleman-Plata*, Opinion and Order, 7.

6. One such unacceptable precedent was the convict lease system of the South after the Civil War, under which African American prisoners were in the custody of private masters who leased them from the state and often allowed them to die of disease and injury while working them to exhaustion. See Alex Lichtenstein, *Twice the Work of Free Labor: The Political Economy of Convict Labor in the New South* (New York: Verso Books, 1996).

7. The term *emergency government* is often used to describe the use of states of emergency by national governments to set up a permanent new administration under guise of an exception to the normal legal order. The same pattern can emerge, as here, within an institutional framework well beneath the level of the nation state. Didier Fassin and Mariella Pandolfi, eds., *Contemporary States of Emergency: The Politics of Military and Humanitarian Interventions* (New York: Zone, 2010).

8. *Coleman-Plata*, Opinion and Order, 58, quoting Doyle Wayne Scott, a thirty-year employee of the Texas Department of Criminal Justice who served as its Executive Director for five years.

9. Ibid., 107, quoting Jeanne Woodford, former secretary of corrections for California and former warden of San Quentin Prison.

10. Ibid., 6.

11. Ibid., 73.

12. Ibid., 94.

13. Ibid., 99, emphasis added.

14. Ibid., 94.

15. It is just as likely that this is a reflection of the lack of civil rights lawyers for prisoners in many parts of the country. Fifteen other states supported California in a friend of the court brief to

the Supreme Court, citing the likelihood that they could face similar crowding problems.

16. Federal policy throughout this period also encouraged longer prison sentences through "truth in sentencing" policies requiring felons to serve 80 percent or more of their stated prison sentence in order for the state to qualify for federal prison funding.

17. The first of these requirements makes it harder for a cap to be created in the first place, for in addition to persuading one judge, who has typically already ruled numerous times in favor of the plaintiffs on key constitutional issues, petitioners must persuade at least two other judges who have not been directly involved. Having an appellate judge may have been intended to place a more legally narrow perspective on the case, because appeals court judges spend less time exposed directly to the evidence of institutional failures and more time applying tricky analytic tests. They are also increasingly likely to have already served as federal trial judges prior to their nomination for the appeals court, which means that the political process of Senate confirmation will be a second opportunity to consider a judge's fealty to crime-control values.

18. *Coleman-Plata*, Opinion and Order, 172.

19. This was Zimring and Hawkins's persuasive critique of incapacitation in 1995. See Franklin Zimring and Gordon Hawkins, *Incapacitation: Penal Confinement and the Restraint of Crime* (New York: Oxford University Press, 1995).

20. In January 2013, the state essentially acknowledged that tens of thousands of prisoners posed little risk to public safety. In a motion to terminate the population reduction plan after reducing the prison population by nearly thirty thousand prisoners, the state claimed that further reductions required to meet the population-cap target of 137 percent of design capacity would pose an unacceptable danger to public safety. Of course, it had made the very same argument in challenging *any* population-reduction plan.

21. *Coleman-Plata*, Opinion and Order, 155.

22. Ibid., 141.

23. Ibid., 63.

24. Recidivism, or the rate at which persons released from prison are sent back, has roughly doubled during the era of total incapacitation in California. See Joan Petersilia, *When Prisoners*

Come Home: Parole and Prison Reentry (New York: Oxford University Press, 2003), 11–13. Recidivism is nonetheless a complex outcome as dependent on overpolicing as it is on crime. Many former prisoners in the era of mass incarceration were returned to prison for minor violations such as using drugs or missing appointments. The routine revocation of parole for such violations is explainable only by the total incapacitation rationale.

25. David Garland called it the "common sense of high crime societies," but now it has little relationship to actual crime rates. See David Garland, *The Culture of Control: Crime and Social Order in Contemporary Society* (Chicago: University of Chicago Press, 2002), 11.

26. The court noted that some fifteen studies had been issued since 1990 containing "essentially the same ten recommendations." *Coleman-Plata*, Opinion and Order, 154, quoting criminologist Joan Petersilia.

27. Ibid., 146.

28. With no apparent irony, California's political leaders have recently mostly embraced rehabilitation as a reason to further delay the mandate of the courts to reduce overcrowding to levels that will relieve the risk of torture. In 2013, nearly thirty years after the original *Coleman* order, Governor Brown and legislative leaders asked the three-judge court for an additional three-year delay, arguing that rehabilitation will reduce overcrowding over three years without requiring the state to release any current prisoners. (Of course the state had long been free to pursue rehabilitation as a way to reduce overcrowding during the years they had already delayed the 2009 *Coleman-Plata* mandate in appeals). Quite appropriately the court rejected this argument, granting only a five-month extension, until April 2014. "Judges Extend State Prison Overcrowding Deadline to April," *News Fix* blog, KQED, December 11, 2013, blogs.kqed.org/newsfix/2013/12/11/California-prison-overcrowding-deadline.

29. Indeed, that exact phrase was used by one of California's leading criminologists, Joan Petersilia of Stanford University. See Joan Petersilia and Jessica Greenlick Snyder, "Looking Past the Hype: 10 Questions Everyone Should Ask About California's Prison Realignment," *California Journal of Politics and Policy* 5, no. 2 (2013): 266–306.

30. As noted by the court, in 2006 California's rate of prison suicide was 45 percent higher than the national average.

31. *Coleman-Plata,* Opinion and Order, 69.

32. Ibid., 182, citing the late constitutional scholar John Hart Ely's *Democracy and Distrust,* a study devoted to explaining the role of the courts in the 1950s through the 1970s, especially in the desegregation arena.

6. *Dignity Cascade:* Brown v. Plata *and Mass Incarceration as a Human Rights Problem*

1. The Supreme Court affirmed the order of a special three-judge court ordering the largest prison population reduction in history, some forty thousand inmates over two years. The three-judge panel gave the state wide discretion to reduce population by any combination of releasing current prisoners and diverting incoming prisoners to jail or other sanction, but required California, which has long enacted policies intended to increase the prison population, to reduce it substantially.

2. Brown v. Plata, 131 S.Ct. 1910, 1928.

3. Ibid., 1925, n. 3.

4. As this goes to press, the state has received the latest of several extensions, giving it until 2016 to reach the target percentage above capacity. The extension comes, however, with an unprecedented agreement by the state to increase the role of early release through parole and to assign a risk assessment to every prisoner such that further population reductions can occur through early release, if necessary, based on factors relevant to public safety.

5. Ibid., quoting Trop v. Dulles, 356 U.S. 86, 100 (1958).

6. Leslie Meltzer Henry, "The Jurisprudence of Dignity," *University of Pennsylvania Law Review* 160 (2010): 169–233. Some, most notably legal historian James Whitman, have argued that the course of U.S. history left our law with a far less significant engagement with dignity than was true of Europe, where the long battle to integrate the aristocracy into a structure of equal national citizenship generated a concept of dignity than was at once substantial in its demand for proper treatment and also available equally to all. America, in contrast, eliminated aristocratic titles but kept slavery for nearly a century after Independence. See James Whitman, *Harsh Justice: Criminal Punishment and the Widen-*

ing Divide Between Europe and the United States (New York: Oxford University Press, 2005).

7. Indeed, for much of the nineteenth century, the major emphasis on dignity involved the dignity of the state.

8. Trop v. Dulles, 356 U.S. 86 (1958).

9. Exemplified in *Spain v. Procunier*'s "dangerous men in safe custody humanely" formula.

10. Michelline Ishay, *The History of Human Rights: From Ancient Times to the Globalization Era* (Berkeley: University of California Press, 2008).

11. *Trop*, 356 U.S. 86, 100.

12. Furman v. Georgia, 408 U.S. 238, 271–73, Brennan concurring.

13. Harmelin v. Michigan, 501 U.S. 957 (1991).

14. The primary vehicle of this respect for human dignity is the Council of Europe, whose members now include virtually every European nation. The human rights organs of this Council include the European Court of Human Rights, the Committee for the Prevention of Torture, and the Committee of Ministers. The primary source of human rights in the Council is the European Convention on Human Rights, which, like the U.S. Constitution, lacks much explicit use of the concept of dignity but nonetheless has given rise to widely accepted norms under the concept of dignity, many of them expressed in the Council of Europe's European Prison Rules (2006), wcd.coe.int/ViewDoc.jsp?id=955747.

15. Dirk van Zyl Smit and Sonja Snacken, *Principles of European Prison Law and Policy: Penology and Human Rights* (New York: Oxford University Press, 2009).

16. Dignity of prisoners anchors a whole set of prisoner rights that can be enforced in most national courts of the European Community member states (as well as in the European Court of Human Rights). In this respect, enforcement parallels that of prisoners' rights by federal courts in the United States. However, in Europe, but not the United States, dignity also informs a body of norms or principles expected to guide the administration of imprisonment in the member states.

17. Which forbids "torture and inhuman or degrading treatment or punishment."

18. When combined into a systemwide population cap, such litigation begins to approach the comprehensive counterpressure human rights institutions do in Europe. With California facing a

decade or more of oversight by the *Coleman* and *Plata* courts, it is as if the jurisdiction has been temporarily placed in the European legal context.

19. Malcolm Feeley and Edward Rubin, *Judicial Policy Making and the Modern State* (Cambridge: Cambridge University Press, 2000).

20. *Brown* at 1925–26.

21. Ibid., 1928.

22. Ibid., 1951, Scalia dissenting.

23. Scalia's logic is breathtaking in its ability to define the Eighth Amendment so as to be irrelevant in an age of chronic illness, just as it would have been in the age of jail fever.

24. Hudson v. Palmer, 468 U.S. 517 (1984); Wilson v. Seiter, 501 U.S. 294 (1991); and Farmer v. Brennan, 511 U.S. 825 (1994).

25. Texas is perhaps the best "managed" version of mass incarceration in America. See Robert Perkinson, *Texas Tough: The Rise of America's Prison Empire* (New York: Picador, 2010).

26. A lot depends on the individual judges who hear prisoner claims in the coming years. As was true during the era of prisoners' rights, judges can easily avoid confronting unconstitutional conditions in prison by deferring to prison administrative judgment. Overcoming this barrier requires a strong sense that the conditions of imprisonment at issue in a specific trial cross a moral boundary. Furthermore, sustaining the court oversight necessary to achieve institutional reform requires the development of broad interpretive norms, which can provide both substantive standards for evaluating prison practices as well as limits to judicial intervention in the affairs of elected state officials. See Feeley and Rubin, *Judicial Policy Making and the Modern State.*

27. In fact, this was largely driven by penal policy in the progressive states bolstered by the drive for national standards carried out by the American Correctional Association (a national professional organization for prison managers) and the Justice Department during those years.

28. This "realism" had three elements: (1) prisoners are an unfathomable and unchangeable threat against social order and the lives of law-abiding citizens; (2) crime is an aggregate product of the presence in society of a high concentration of criminals; and (3) prison is a regrettable but necessary and certainly humane

way to remove a sufficient number of criminals from society to achieve a tolerable level of public safety.

29. The suffering of people in New Orleans during the flood that followed Hurricane Katrina is one U.S. example that offers some interesting parallels to the prison crisis in *Brown*.

30. Didier Fassin, *Humanitarian Reason: A Moral History of the Present* (Berkeley: University of California Press, 2012).

31. Schwarzenegger (later Brown after Governor Jerry Brown took over in January 2011) v. Plata, 2010 WL 4859507 (U.S.) (Oral Argument), 19, 26.

32. Jonathan Simon, "The Return of the Medical Model: Disease and the Meaning of Imprisonment from John Howard to *Brown v. Plata*," *Harvard Civil Rights–Civil Liberties Law Review* 48, no. 1 (Winter 2013): 217–56.

33. Ibid.

34. For example, the United States helped draft the Universal Declaration of Human Rights while blocking efforts to link the human rights charter to the struggle against Jim Crow in the United States itself. See Carole Anderson, *Eyes Off the Prize: The United Nations and the African American Struggle for Human Rights, 1944–1955* (New York: Cambridge University Press, 2003).

35. Brown v. Plata, 131 S.Ct. 1910, 1923, 1960.

36. *Brown*, 1951, emphasis added by author.

37. *Brown*, 1968.

38. Ibid., 1943.

39. Madrid v. Gomez, 889 F.Supp. 1146 (N.D. Cal. 1995).

7. The New Common Sense of High-Crime Societies

1. Trop v. Dulles (1958) 356 U.S. 86; Furman v. George (1972) 408 U.S. 238, discussed in chapter 6.

2. I mean by this only that we are and have been for some time a society that understands itself as having a lot of crime, but we have also become a society that understands itself as having a lot of—in fact too much—incarceration.

3. Such windows are invariably open for a short time. See John W. Kingdon, *Agendas, Alternatives and Public Policies*, 2nd ed. (New York: Longman, 2003), 88.

4. An influential academic statement of this perspective is John DiIulio, *Governing Prisons: A Comparative Study of Correctional Management* (New York: The Free Press, 1990).

5. The term was most notably used by William Bennett, John DiIulio, and John Walters in their much discussed (and now criticized) book *Body Count: How to Win America's War Against Crime and Drugs* (New York: Simon & Schuster, 1996).

6. Indeed I believe the record will show that boomers played an outsize role in shaping the new common sense; see, e.g., the work of Eric Cadora, Angela Davis, Ruth Gilmore, Judith Green, Marc Mauer, Joan Petersilia, Jeremy Travis, Susan Tucker, as well as of lawyers such as Michael Bien and Donald Specter.

7. See, for example, the recommendations to limit the prison population in the report of the President's Commission on Law Enforcement and the Administration of Justice, Nicholas Katzenbach, chairman, *The Challenge of Crime in a Free Society* (Washington, DC: Government Printing Office, 1967), www.ncjrs.gov/pdffiles1/nij/42.pdf.

8. Recommendation 23 of the Rules of Prisons drawn up by the Council of Europe's Committee of Ministers, which concerns the protection of the human dignity of those undergoing long-term imprisonment, draws the lower boundary of that status at five years. In the United States, the proliferation of extreme sentences has made five years sound modest.

9. Many states are adopting compassionate parole laws, but implementation has been far too slow and grudging.

10. Robert J. Sampson and John H. Laub, *Crime in the Making: Pathways and Turning Points Through Life* (Cambridge, MA: Harvard University Press, 1993) is the modern classic.

11. Franklin Zimring, *The City That Became Safe: New York's Lessons for Urban Crime and Its Reduction* (New York: Oxford University Press, 2011).

12. Richard Florida, *Who's Your City? How the Creative Economy Is Making Where You Live the Most Important Decision of Your Life* (New York: Vintage, 2010).

13. Malcolm M. Feeley and Jonathan Simon, "The New Penology: Notes on the Emerging Strategy of Corrections and Its Implications," *Criminology* 30, no. 4 (1992): 449–74.

14. Zimring, *City That Became Safe*; and David Kennedy, *Don't*

Shoot: One Man, a Street Fellowship, and the End of Violence in Inner City America (New York: Bloomsbury, 2012).

15. See, for example, Merith Cosden, Jeffrey K. Ellens, Jeffrey L. Schnell, Yasmeen Yamini-Diouf, and Maren M. Wolfe, "Evaluation of a Mental Health Treatment Court with Assertive Community Treatment," *Behavioral Sciences and the Law* 21, no. 4 (2003): 415–27.

16. Jeremy Travis, *But They All Come Back: Facing the Challenge of Prisoner Reentry* (New York: Urban Institute, 2005).

17. Micheline R. Ishay, *The History of Human Rights: From Ancient Times to the Globalization Era* (Berkeley: University of California Press, 2008).

18. Miranda v. Arizona, 384 U.S. 436 (1966); and Mapp v. Ohio, 367 U.S. 643 (1961).

19. O'Connor v. Donaldson, 422 U.S. 563 (1975).

20. For a recent report, see Andrew Cohen, "One of the Darkest Periods in the History of American Prisons," *Atlantic Monthly*, June 9, 2013.

21. Ruti G. Teitel, *Transitional Justice* (New Haven, CT: Yale University Press 2002).

22. Dirk van Zyl Smit and Sonja Snacken, *Principles of European Prison Law and Policy: Penology and Human Rights* (New York: Oxford University Press, 2013).

Index

Publishing in the Public Interest

Thank you for reading this book published by The New Press. The New Press is a nonprofit, public interest publisher. New Press books and authors play a crucial role in sparking conversations about the key political and social issues of our day.

We hope you enjoyed this book and that you will stay in touch with The New Press. Here are a few ways to stay up to date with our books, events, and the issues we cover:

- Sign up at www.thenewpress.com/subscribe to receive updates on New Press authors and issues and to be notified about local events
- Like us on Facebook: www.facebook.com/newpressbooks
- Follow us on Twitter: www.twitter.com/thenewpress

Please consider buying New Press books for yourself; for friends and family; or to donate to schools, libraries, community centers, prison libraries, and other organizations involved with the issues our authors write about.

The New Press is a 501(c)(3) nonprofit organization. You can also support our work with a tax-deductible gift by visiting www.thenewpress.com/donate.